SEPHARDI VOICES

SEPHARDI VOICES

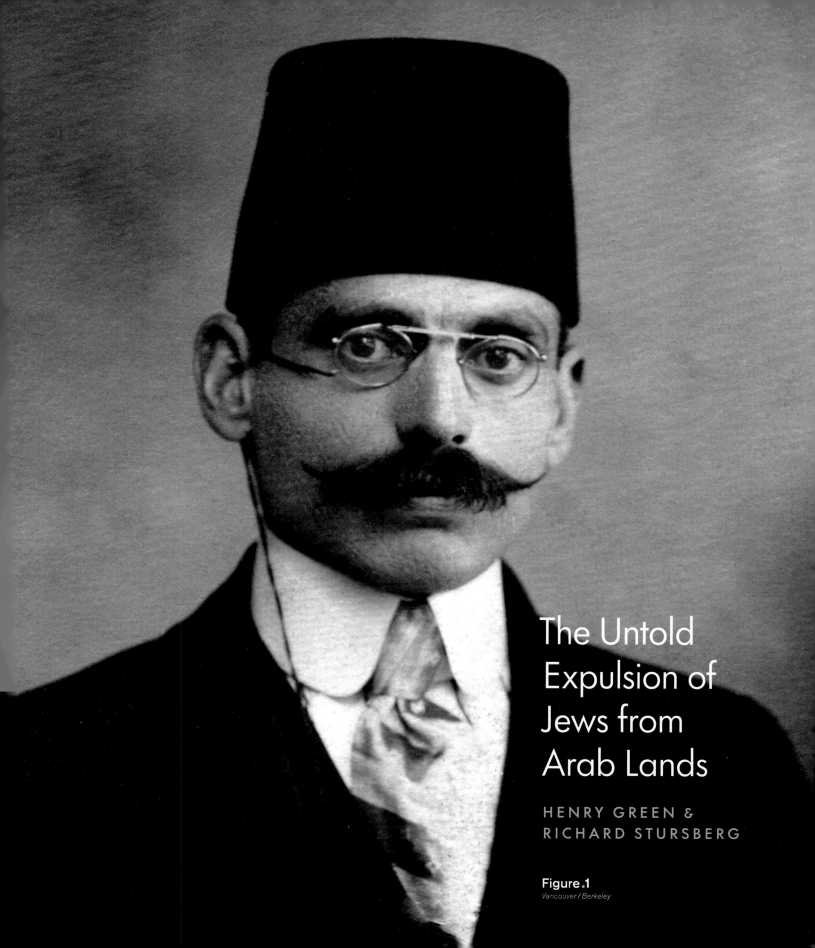

The Untold Expulsion of Jews from Arab Lands

HENRY GREEN &
RICHARD STURSBERG

Figure.1
Vancouver / Berkeley

Cataloguing data is available from Library and Archives Canada
ISBN 978-1-77327-153-8 (hbk.)

Design by Naomi MacDougall

Photo Editor: David Langer
Archives Editor: Zoë Lepiano
Research Archivist: Rebecca Lash
Research Assistant: Leslie Benaudis

Editing by Michael Leyne
Copy editing by Pam Robertson
Proofreading by Renate Preuss
Indexing by Stephen Ullstrom

Front cover photograph top right courtesy of the Central Zionist Archives.
All others from the Sephardi Voices archive.
Back cover photographs from the Sephardi Voices archive.
Author photos by Vincent DeVries (Henry Green) and
Yuula Benivolski (Richard Stursberg)

Printed and bound in China by C&C Offset Printing Co.
Distributed internationally by Publishers Group West

Figure 1 Publishing Inc.
Vancouver BC Canada
www.figure1publishing.com

TITLE PAGE IMAGE:
Meir Daniel, Istanbul,
Turkey, 1914
Courtesy of Robert Mashaal

DEDICATED TO THE MEMORY OF
SIR NAIM AND RENÉE DANGOOR

A Yemeni family walking
through the desert
with a Torah scroll to
a reception camp
near Aden, 1949

CONTENTS

INTRODUCTION
1

1 ANCIENT HOMELANDS
7

2 THE ARAB JEWS BEFORE ISRAEL
19

3 THE EXODUS BEGINS: 1948–1967
51

4 THE EXODUS CONTINUES: 1967–1980
85

5 TODAY AND TOMORROW
105

SEPHARDI FACES
PORTRAIT GALLERY
127

ACKNOWLEDGMENTS
138

GLOSSARY
141

NOTES
145

RECOMMENDED READINGS, MEDIA, AND MUSEUMS
147

INDEX
151

ABOUT THE AUTHORS
156

INTRODUCTION

JEWS HAVE LIVED in the Middle East and North Africa since time immemorial. Known by various names, such as Babylonian, Persian, Sephardi, Arab, or Mizrahi Jews, their presence predated the arrival of Islam by more than two millennia.* They have one of the longest, continuous written histories of any people on the planet. Many of the key building blocks of Western civilization were invented by these ancient Jews, including the origin stories of Judaism, Christianity, and Islam: the creation of the earth in six days, Adam and Eve, the Garden of Eden, the Flood, and the Ten Commandments. They created monotheism and its contemporary manifestations in the words of Jesus and Muhammad.

With the arrival of Islam in the seventh century CE and the conquest by early caliphates of Persia, Palestine, most of the Middle East, North Africa, and the Iberian Peninsula, the Sephardi Jews found themselves the subjects of Muslim rulers. They became—like the Christians—second-class citizens, but were still

▲◄ Jewish woman from
Agdz, Morocco, c. 1935
Photo: Jean Besancenot / © 2021
Artists Rights Society (ARS), New York /
ADAGP, Paris

▲ Jewish man from Zagora,
Morocco, c. 1935
Photo: Jean Besancenot / © 2021
Artists Rights Society (ARS), New York /
ADAGP, Paris

---

* See the glossary (p. 141) for more on these terms.

respected as "People of the Book." Their situation varied from place to place. In parts of the Muslim empire they prospered; in other parts, they suffered discrimination. But nowhere did they fare as badly during the Middle Ages as the Jews of Europe.

The Jews of North Africa and the Middle East continued to live in their ancestral homelands until the end of the World War II. Then, with the rise of Arab nationalism and the founding of the State of Israel, their Muslim neighbors turned against them. Their governments seized their property, imprisoned their leaders, stripped them of their citizenship, and forced them to flee the places where they had lived for millennia—and to become refugees in North America, Israel, and Europe.

The plight of the Palestinian refugees in the War of Independence in 1948 is well known. Roughly 725,000 people lost their villages, farms, homes, and businesses. The United Nations set up a dedicated agency to assist them. Their situation has been the subject of global concern for seventy years.

The story of the Sephardi Jewish refugees is much less well known. Where there were close to 850,000 Jews in the Middle East and North Africa after World War II, by 2021 there were less than 4,000. No UN agency was established to assist them, and no countries demanded justice for them. Their displacement and dispossession was largely ignored by the international community.

In 2009, the Sephardi Voices International (SVI) project was launched to document the lives of those who had to leave their ancient homes, and preserve, as best it can, the stories of their ancient cultures and of peoples that will soon be gone forever. The SVI digital audiovisual collection is the largest of its kind in the world. To date, over 450 interviews have been done, recording what life was like for the Jews living in Arab lands and Iran, what happened to the individuals who had to flee, and what has become of them since. The SVI Archive contains not only the interviews, but also family photographs, school report cards, passports, property deeds, identity cards, and souvenirs, a vast assemblage of materials from the world that was lost. It is housed in the Sephardi Voices International website and the National Library of Israel.

Sephardi Voices: The Untold Expulsion of Jews from Arab Lands draws on this extraordinary collection to tell the story of this catastrophe. It does so through the words of the people who lived through it. They describe their lives before the expulsions began, the terror they had to endure, and the ways in which they rebuilt in the countries that embraced them. The book includes many of their family photographs and portraits. There are rare and privileged glimpses into their schools, family gatherings, marriages, and celebrations. They appear as they were then—in Baghdad, Cairo, and Algiers—and as they are now. Their stories are stories of loss, but also stories of redemption.

WHO ARE THE SEPHARDI?

In the strictest sense, "Sephardi" Jews (from *Sephard*, or "Spanish," in modern Hebrew) are those who trace their roots to the Iberian Peninsula or to the descendants of those Jews, who settled in the Mediterranean basin or in countries of the Ottoman Empire after the expulsion from Spain and who preserved Spanish ways and the Judaeo-Spanish language after their exile in 1492.

There were a great many Sephardi communities. Their sheer variety and complexity makes it difficult to generalize about them. Historically, many spoke Arabic in public places (to avoid being identified as Jews) and Judaeo-Arabic (which had many dialects) at home. Others spoke variations of Spanish, like Haketia (in Spanish Morocco) or Ladino (in the Ottoman Empire).

With the founding of the State of Israel in 1948, a new term was constructed: "Mizrahi" (from "Eastern" in Hebrew), which collectively refers to non-Western Jews, and distinguishes them from Ashkenazi Jews—those from Western countries who lived in Christian lands.

Jews who have lived in Iraq and Iran (Babylon and Mesopotamia) since the destruction of the First Temple (587 BCE) view themselves as neither Sephardi nor Mizrahi but as Babylonian and Persian, but nonetheless are lumped into the Mizrahi category by Israelis.

The Jews of the Maghreb historically spoke Arabic (and Judaeo-Arabic) and shared Arabic culture with their Muslim neighbors. With the colonization of North Africa by France, however, the Jews of Tunisia, Algeria, and Morocco began to speak French and grew increasingly westernized. By the beginning of the twentieth century, they identified themselves as Tunisian-French Jews, Algerian-French Jews and Moroccan-French Jews.

Similarly in Libya, although the Jews of the nineteenth century spoke Arabic, the takeover of the country by Italy meant that they began to speak Italian. Like the other Jews of the Maghreb, they became increasingly Europeanized culturally.

More broadly, and with the exception of the Persian Jews, the terms "Sephardi" and "Mizrahi" have come to mean Jews who shared a common heritage, culture, and language with their Arab neighbors. Sometimes they identify themselves as "Arab Jews." Many others, however, dislike the term "Arab Jews," since it reminds them of their expulsion from their homes in the Arab lands. Throughout this book we use the terms "Sephardi Jews" and "Arab Jews" interchangeably, except when we discuss the situation of the Persian Jews.

The Sephardi and Persian Jews have, for the most part, common *halakhah* (laws), *minhag* (customs), and cultural norms. They eat rice for Passover, for instance, in contrast to the Ashkenazi, who view it as forbidden. In synagogues in North Africa, the Middle East, and Iran, the normative practice is reading Torah while it is vertically upright on a table rather than placed horizontally, as is the practice in Ashkenazi synagogues.

THE VOICES OF this book include those who self-identify as Sephardi, Mizrahi, Babylonian, Arab, and Persian. Many of these individuals share a language, a culture, and religious practices, and all were displaced from North Africa, the Middle East, or Iran. Their story is told historically. It begins with the first Jew, Abraham, and moves forward through the vast reaches of Jewish history—the kingdoms, the exiles, and the defeats—to the emergence of Arab nationalism and Zionism in the late nineteenth and early twentieth centuries. It describes the terrible and deadly tensions between these two opposed ideologies. And it works its way through the great events of the postwar period: the founding of the State of Israel and the War of Independence, the Suez Crisis, the Algerian Revolution, the Six-Day War, the Yom Kippur War, and the Iranian Revolution.

These events are seen and heard through the voices of the displaced. There are wealthy bankers and businessmen from Baghdad, friends of the last king of Egypt, impoverished artisans from the Casbah in Algiers, mountain peasants from Morocco, intellectuals and Nobel prize winners, schoolgirls in Yemen, daring smugglers, and influential politicians. There are witnesses to the pogroms in Libya and Egypt, the burning of the synagogues in Syria, the terrible Farhud in Iraq; there are passengers on the great airlifts of the Magic Carpet and Operation Ezra and Nehemiah; there are families escaping through the mountains of Kurdistan into Iran; there are husbands smuggled in carpets into Iran in search of wives. There are fortunes rebuilt in London and New York; there are novels written and Nobel prizes won.

The story of the Sephardi Jewish displacement is, of course, not just a story about a vanishing set of rich cultures and peoples. It is also a story of human rights. It is a story of not just what was lost to the Jews, but what was lost to the Arab countries that expelled them. It is a story of what might have been if those countries had retained and treasured these gifted citizens.

SEPHARDI VOICES

ANCIENT HOMELANDS

"And I will establish my covenant between
me and you, and your descendants after
you in their generations . . . and I will
give unto you, and your descendants,
the land of your sojournings."

GENESIS 17:7–8

1 JEWS HAVE LIVED IN THE MIDDLE EAST and North Africa since at least 2000 BCE. Their history covers many of the greatest events of the Jewish narrative: they were the people released from bondage by Moses, the people who founded Jerusalem and built the First Temple. They later saw Jerusalem sacked and the First Temple destroyed, and they were exiled into Babylon. When they returned, they rebuilt the temple, the Second Temple, only to later see Judea conquered by the Romans, and they once again dispersed.

Abraham, the first Jew, arrived in Canaan (in present-day Israel) from Ur in Iraq 4,000 years ago. God made Abraham a promise:

> And when Abram was ninety years old and nine, the Lord appeared to Abram and said to him, I am the Almighty God; walk before me and be thou wholehearted. And I will make my covenant between me and thee, and I will multiply thee exceedingly. And Abram fell on his face; and God talked with him saying:

"I have delivered you out of the hand of the Egyptians . . . know that the Lord is greater than all gods."
EXODUS 18:9-13

Damaged Torah scroll recovered by the U.S. Army from the Mukhabarat, Saddam Hussein's intelligence headquarters, 2003
Photo: Raphael Abada

A mosaic in the sixth-century CE Beth Alpha Synagogue near Beit She'an, Israel
The Picture Art Collection / Alamy Stock Photo

As for me, behold, my covenant is with thee and thou shalt be a father of a multitude of nations. Neither shall thy name any more be called Abram; but thy name shall be Abraham, for a father of a multitude of nations have I made thee. (Genesis 17:1–5) [1]

God was as good as his word. Abraham and his lineage anchor the three great monotheistic religions of the West:

- Judaism
- Christianity, with Jesus of Nazareth descended from Abraham's son Isaac
- Islam, with the prophet Muhammad descended from Abraham's son Ishmael

Seven hundred years after Abraham, Moses led the people of Israel out of bondage and slavery in Egypt. The waters parted to let the Israelites cross the sea and then closed, drowning Pharaoh's army. Moses spoke with God. He received the Ten Commandments. After forty years in the wilderness, the Israelites were delivered into the promised land that God had bequeathed to Abraham.

Centuries later, the Israelite monarchy emerged under King Saul and then King David (c. 1000 BCE), a member of the tribe of Judah. David founded a new city, Jerusalem, and his son, Solomon, built the First Temple (c. 950 BCE).

These 1,000 years of Jewish history generated the foundations of Western civilization. The myths of creation, the stories of Adam and Eve, Noah and the

This page from the Sarajevo Haggadah, an illuminated manuscript created in Barcelona in the fourteenth century, depicts Moses parting the Red Sea and leading the Israelites out of Egypt.
Bible Land Pictures / Alamy Stock Photo

Ark, the Tower of Babel, Moses and the Exodus, David and Goliath, the Wisdom of Solomon, and the story of Job, are touchstones of Western thought and art. The Jews of the period collected these stories into the Torah, the five books of Moses, and the Prophets and Writings (the Tanakh), which became the foundation of the Christian Old Testament.

In 587 BCE, the Babylonians invaded Judea (Israel). It was as Jeremiah and Ezekiel had prophesied: "And this whole land shall be waste and desolation and an astonishment; and these nations shall serve the King of Babylon seventy years." (Jeremiah 25:11)[2]

The forces of Nebuchadnezzar sacked Jerusalem and destroyed and looted the First Temple built by Solomon. This was followed by waves of deportations, during which the Jews were sent into exile in Babylon (present-day Iraq).

The exile was not to last forever, as Jeremiah assured the Israelites: "For so said the Lord: For at the completion of seventy years of Babylon I will remember you, and … restore you to this place. For I know the thoughts that I think about you, says the Lord, thoughts of peace and not of evil, to give you a future with hope." (Jeremiah 29:10–11)

Ezekiel confirmed God's promise: "And they shall know that I am the Lord their God, in that I caused them to go into captivity among the nations, and have gathered them unto their own land; and I will leave none of them any more there; neither will I hide My face any more from them; for I have poured out My spirit upon the house of Israel." (Ezekiel 39:28–29)

▶ This detail from a bas-relief sculpture removed from Sennacherib's "Palace Without Rival" in Nineveh, Iraq, (now in the British Museum) depicts deportees after the Assyrian siege of Lachish, Judea (701 BCE).

▼ Painting (tempera on plaster) depicting Ezekiel's prophecy, from the third-century CE Dura-Europos Synagogue in Syria, which was relocated to the National Museum of Damascus in the 1930s

The exile turned Iraq into the center of Jewish thought and scholarship for the next 1,400 years. It is there that the Jews completed the Talmud (c. 475 CE), the great work of wisdom that describes the laws, interpretations, and customs that govern Jewish life to the present day.

Seventy years later, Cyrus the Great, the king of Persia (present-day Iran), reversed the orders of Nebuchadnezzar and told the Jews to return to Jerusalem and rebuild the temple: "Thus said Cyrus king of Persia: All the kingdoms of the earth has the Lord, the God of heaven, given me; and He has charged me to build Him a house in Jerusalem, which is in Judah." (Ezra 1:2)

To ensure that full reparations were made, Cyrus enjoined all his subjects to assist the Jews in the rebuilding of the temple. He also returned what Nebuchadnezzar had looted: "Also Cyrus the king brought forth the vessels of the house of the Lord, which Nebuchadnezzar had brought forth out of Jerusalem, and had put them in the house of his gods... All these did Sheshbazzar bring up, when they of the captivity were brought up from Babylon unto Jerusalem." (Ezra 1:7,11)

Ezra left Babylon, along with the prophet Nehemiah and the captured Jews, to oversee the construction of the Second Temple and the new walls around the city of Jerusalem.

Roughly 150 years later, Alexander the Great, the Greek king of Macedonia, conquered a vast swath of the world. His empire stretched through the Fertile

▲◀ Ruins of Babylon,
Iraq, 1932
*Underwood Archives / UIG /
Bridgeman Images*

▲ Iraqi Jews at Ezekiel's
Tomb, Al Kifl, Iraq, 1932
*Prints and Photographs Collection,
Library of Congress, LC-M33-14508*

Crescent and North Africa as far east as the Indus Valley. He established Alexandria in northern Egypt on the shores of the Mediterranean. Alexandria became the capital of learning in the ancient world.

Although the city was Greek and became the capital of the Ptolemaic Kingdom, Jews were prominent citizens and occupied a special quarter near the royal palace and the Great Library. It is here that the Torah was translated from Hebrew into Greek—the new version being called the Septuagint—making it available to be read throughout literate Europe.

Two hundred years later, the Roman Empire rose to take over large areas of the world that were home to substantial Jewish populations. Huge tracts of North Africa came under Roman control. Present-day Morocco, Tunisia, Algeria, Libya, and Egypt were all Roman provinces by 75 BCE.

In 63 BCE, the Romans conquered Judea, the homeland of the Jews, ending the independence of the Jewish kingdom and setting in motion the emergence of the second great monotheistic religion, Christianity. Jesus, a Jew, was born some sixty years later, in humble circumstances in Bethlehem. He contended with the Jewish elders in the Second Temple, preaching and performing miracles. He attracted disciples and followers, many of whom were fishermen working in the Sea of Galilee. Ultimately, he was arrested by the Romans and crucified in Jerusalem for subversion.

His story became the second great pillar of Western thought and culture. The virgin birth, walking on water, the sermon on the mount, the raising of the dead, the crucifixion and his resurrection—these became the central parables of European art and philosophy for the next 2,000 years. Jesus was, however, repudiated by the Jews, who themselves would be blamed for his death at the hands of the Romans by future Christians. With the rise of the Catholic church, Jews were vilified and falsely attacked as the "Killers of Christ."

In 66 CE, the Jews in Israel rose up against their Roman overlords. Four years later, Jerusalem fell to the Roman army and the Second Temple was destroyed. As punishment, thousands of Jews were expelled from Judea to provinces in North Africa, the Middle East, and Italy. Slightly more than sixty years later, the Jews rebelled again in Judea. The Bar Kokhba revolt spelled the effective end of the Jewish presence in Jerusalem for the next 400 years, and led to a new name for the region, Syria Palaestina, introduced circa 135 CE by the Roman emperor Hadrian. This time the Romans did not simply expel the Jews. They killed the men in large numbers and sold the women and children into slavery. Those who could, fled, principally to Iraq and Egypt.

With the breakup of the Roman Empire, Jerusalem and Palestine became part of the Byzantine Empire, which was Christian. The empire's policy from the fifth century onward was to convert the Jews to Christianity. Those who failed to convert were persecuted.

Muhammad (c. 570– c. 632 CE) and the Archangel Gabriel, from the *Siyer-i Nebi*, the fourteenth-century Turkish epic
Topkapi Palace Museum, Istanbul, Turkey Bildarchiv, Steffens / Bridgeman Images

The Persians conquered Jerusalem in 614 CE and encouraged the Jews to return, almost 550 years after their expulsion by the Romans. Unfortunately, when the Persians left in 629 CE and the city was returned to the Byzantine Empire, Christian radicals massacred the Jews, who fled again to Egypt. It would be more than 1,300 years before Jerusalem again came under Jewish control.

In 570 CE, the prophet Muhammad was born. He was, according to the Koran, sent by God to preach and confirm the monotheistic prophecies of Abraham, David, and Jesus. He claimed descent from Ishmael, Abraham's first born, and promised the final revelation of God's truth. Muhammad taught respect for the other People of the Book, the Christians and Jews. He urged the Jews to accept him as the new Prophet and become Muslims. The Jews rejected his advances, causing him to draw ever sharper distinctions between their beliefs and those of Islam.

In 622 CE, the tensions between Muhammad and the Jews burst into open warfare. The forces of Islam defeated the Jews at Medina in today's Saudi Arabia, and 700 Jewish men were beheaded and thrown into an open pit. All the Jewish males who had not yet reached puberty, along with the women and girls, were sold into slavery.

Maimonides teaches students about the "measure of man" in this page from the "Copenhagen Maimonides," illuminated by Ferrer Bassa in the fourteenth century.

A final battle took place at Khaibar in 628 CE. The terms of the Jews' surrender set the precedent for how they were to be treated in future. They had to surrender half their harvest and give their land over to the Muslim community. The Jews were to be kept in a state of submission and fealty in perpetuity in Ishmael's house.

The new position of the Jews in the Islamic world was as *dhimmi*, the term for non-Muslims living in an Islamic state with legal protection. As People of the Book, they enjoyed only second-class status and were considered inferior to the Muslims. They also had to pay the jizya tax, a tax higher than the ones that were paid by the followers of the Prophet. The Covenant of Omar, which codified the rules of *dhimmi* status, also provided, among other requirements, that no new synagogues could be built; that Jews could not ride horses, only donkeys; that they could only ride sidesaddle; and that they had to wear special hats, cloaks, and shoes to distinguish them from Muslims.

The Covenant of Omar was enforced to varying degrees in different times and places. What *dhimmi* status meant as a practical matter could vary from almost nothing to extremely repressive regulations of suffocating and sometimes deadly cruelty. In early Muslim Spain (eighth century), for example, the Sephardi Jews prospered for almost 400 years, able to practice their religion and enjoy the same basic rights as Muslims. Maimonides—the great Torah scholar, physician, and astronomer—was born there. The Iberian Peninsula became a center of Jewish learning, commerce, and art.

In Mamluk Egypt, however, the *dhimmi* regulations were enforced with rigor. Jews could not serve as public officials or ride horses. For long periods of time, their synagogues were closed completely. In other places, Jews were subject to attack by Muslim mobs, who often killed them, stole their property, and expelled the ones who were left from their homes. They were, in many cases, falsely charged with defiling the Prophet, a crime punishable by death.

The nature of *dhimmi* status defined the relationship between the Sephardi Jews living in the Islamic world and their Muslim neighbors for the 1,300 years that transpired between the founding of the Muslim empire to the Jews' departure from the Arab world after the end of World War II. Where it was lightly enforced, Jews prospered; where it was harshly enforced, Jews suffered.

The mixed attitude of the Muslim world to Jews was not shared in medieval Christian Europe. There, Jews were subject to constant massacres and expulsions.

They were the "Killers of Christ" and it was the duty of good Christians to treat them accordingly. The Crusades saw the beginning of the pogroms that were to plague Europe over the next 1,000 years. As the waves of Crusaders made their way to the Holy Land, they murdered Jews, destroyed their property, and engaged in campaigns of rape and terror.

Following the Crusades, the Jews were expelled from England (1290), France (1394), Hungary (1360), Austria (1421), Spain (1492), and Portugal (1497). The Europeans wanted them gone because they believed that Jews poisoned wells, carried disease, and, worst of all, murdered Christian children to use their blood at Passover (the false claim became known as the "blood libel"). Whatever their second-class status in Arab lands, their position in Europe was almost always much worse.

Throughout the Middle Ages, the Orthodox Christian Byzantine Empire continued to persecute the Jews that lived within its borders, which stretched, at its height, across contemporary Turkey and much of Persia, Iraq, Syria, Lebanon, and Greece. The Jews were often subject to forcible conversions, denied the opportunity to serve in the army or the civil service, and occasionally attacked or forced to live in segregated neighborhoods. The policy of successive governments was to force them to live in a state of absolute humiliation.

The Byzantine Empire came to an end in 1453 when the Ottomans conquered Constantinople. Over the next hundred years the Ottoman Empire was extended to include Iran, Iraq, Palestine, and parts of Saudi Arabia, Egypt, North Africa, Greece, Bulgaria, and Hungary. The emergence of the Ottoman Empire created a marked improvement in the situation of the Jews. Although they were still *dhimmi*, the terms of their status were more tolerant. They still had to pay higher taxes and could not ride horses or carry weapons, but they were able to own property and manage their own communities, including their own schools, synagogues, and cultural organizations. As the Ottoman Empire expanded into more and more Christian lands, the situation of the Jews improved accordingly. In many cases, the Ottoman armies were supported by Jewish fighters keen to throw off the violent anti-Semitism of the Orthodox and Roman Catholic Churches.

The Ottoman Empire lasted for more than 450 years. By the end, however, revolts by the Arabs and colonial interventions by the great European powers had reduced it significantly. France conquered Algeria in 1830 and Tunisia in 1881. The British for their part took Egypt in 1882 and Iraq during World War I.

One of Maimonides's commentaries on the Mishnah, the first major work of Rabbinic Judaism. Avot 8:14
The Picture Art Collection / Alamy Stock Photo

▶ The inaugural congress of the Zionist Organization, convened and chaired by Theodor Herzl, met in Basel, Switzerland, in August 1897.
Universal History Archive / UIG / Bridgeman Images

▶▼ A commemorative postcard of the First Zionist Congress
Photo © Andrusier / Bridgeman Images

By the late nineteenth century, European attitudes toward the Jews had shifted considerably. The states had become increasingly secular, identifying in many cases more with their imperial ambitions than their historic religions. Although anti-Semitism remained a problem, the colonial presence of France and Britain resulted in a significant improvement in the condition of the Jews.

Within the remains of the Ottoman Empire, reform was also taking place in many of its territories. *Dhimmi* status was abolished through the Tanzimat reforms. Although Jews now enjoyed full civil status, Muslim attacks continued sporadically, with many still determined to maintain the second-class status of their Jewish neighbors.

In the late nineteenth century, Zionism emerged as a response to continued anti-Semitism in Europe, and its ideology later resonated throughout the Arab-Jewish world. Its goal was to create a Jewish homeland in the ancestral lands of their forefathers, Israel (Palestine), where Jews could live free of the centuries of persecution they had suffered throughout the world.

The rise of Zionism occurred at about the same time as the rise of Arab nationalism. In the early twentieth century, Arab intellectuals in Paris and Damascus began demanding the creation of Arab nations free from both European colonialism and the Turkish suzerainty of the previous 400 years. They saw Arab nations extending throughout the Middle East and North Africa, including Palestine.

Arab nationalism and Zionism had irreconcilable goals. Many of the elite Sephardi Jews warned that the Zionist project would inflame tensions with their Muslim and Christian Arab neighbors. Poorer Sephardi Jews often saw the Zionist project through a messianic lens and as the great hope for a new and free beginning. They were both right.

A young Jewish woman in traditional costume, Algeria, 1920s
Musée d'art et d'histoire du Judaïsme

By the beginning of the twentieth century, there was a large Jewish population scattered throughout North Africa and the Middle East. They had been in some of the countries for thousands of years and in others for hundreds. In almost all cases, they had been there long before the emergence of Islam. They were distinguishable from their neighbors by their religion and *dhimmi* status, but culturally very similar. Their dress codes, food, and language were more or less the same. They overwhelmingly spoke Arabic. For this reason, they are often referred to as the Arab Jews.

As Tim Mackintosh-Smith has explained, what it means to be an Arab is to speak and read Arabic: "Language is … its defining feature and its genius … the rich, strange, subtle, suavely hypnotic, magically persuasive, maddeningly difficult 'high' Arabic." [3] Many of the Jews in the Middle East and North Africa saw themselves as Arabs, sharing with the rest of the Arab world the great gift and treasure of Arabic. The extreme irony is that despite the closeness of their cultural ties, the twentieth century would bring a terrible reckoning for both the Arab Jews and their host countries. It is often within families that disputes are most bitter.

THE ARAB JEWS
BEFORE ISRAEL

"I'm a Jew, an Arab Jew . . .
I feel very proud of what I am."

EZRA ZILKHA

French Protectorat
identity card for Abraham
Meghira, born 1888,
Safi, Morocco
Courtesy of Edmond Elbaz

2 BETWEEN 1918 AND 1945, the situation of the Arab Jews improved considerably. The Ottoman Empire collapsed and the great European powers with colonies in North Africa and the Middle East—Britain, France, and Italy—strengthened their control and took over countries that had previously been independent. As they did so, they lifted the Jews' *dhimmi* status, strengthening their rights and expanding their ability to participate fully in the cultural, social, and economic life of their countries.

While these were welcome changes for the Jews, they were met with great bitterness by the Muslim Arabs. Where they believed they had been promised independence by the great powers, they perceived instead betrayal. Inevitably, this fanned the flames of Arab nationalism and laid the basis for the catastrophic expulsions of the Jews that began after the end of World War II.

During World War I, the Ottomans allied themselves with Germany. They did so because they needed to modernize their armed forces and because none of the

Ottoman soldiers prepare
to attack British forces
during World War I,
Palestine, 1917.
World History Archive / Alamy Stock Photo

other great powers would have them. It would prove a historic mistake. As the war ground on, the British picked off various parts of the empire. They took Baghdad in 1917 and then captured Tel Aviv and Jerusalem. At the same time, resurgent Arab nationalists fought on the side of Britain hoping to throw off the Turkish yoke and, as a reward, have the English create Arab states.

In Palestine, Jews committed to the Zionist cause had been buying up land since the late nineteenth century and pressing the British government to endorse the creation of a Jewish state there. In 1917, the British cabinet released the Balfour Declaration, in which it committed itself to a Jewish homeland in Palestine. British policy was contradictory, however. It had promised the Arabs a state, which the Arabs, not surprisingly, thought should include Palestine. At the same time, they had given Palestine to the Jews. This contradictory policy sowed the seeds of the next 100 years of anger, war, and suffering.

With the defeat of Germany, World War I came to an end and along with it, the Ottoman Empire. In 1919, France, Britain, and the United States sat down in Paris as victors carving up the spoils. Despite King Faisal (the king of Syria and later of Iraq) arguing for an independent Arab state, Britain was given Iraq and France received Lebanon and much of Syria, while Palestine was made an international protectorate under a British mandate. Some believed that Jordan

▲ Soldiers of the Jewish
Legion (דודגה ירבעה) of
World War I, who fought
for Britain in Egypt and in
Palestine, 1918
Courtesy of the Central Zionist Archives

◄ This World War I
recruiting poster shows a
soldier cutting the bonds
of a Jewish man, who says,
"You have cut my bonds
and set me free—now let
me help you set others
free!"
Library of Congress, Prints and
Photographs Division, LC-USZC4-11300

Foreign Office,
November 2nd, 1917.

Dear Lord Rothschild,

I have much pleasure in conveying to you, on
behalf of His Majesty's Government, the following
declaration of sympathy with Jewish Zionist aspirations
which has been submitted to, and approved by, the Cabinet.

"His Majesty's Government view with favour the
establishment in Palestine of a national home for the
Jewish people, and will use their best endeavours to
facilitate the achievement of this object, it being
clearly understood that nothing shall be done which
may prejudice the civil and religious rights of
existing non-Jewish communities in Palestine, or the
rights and political status enjoyed by Jews in any
other country".

I should be grateful if you would bring this
declaration to the knowledge of the Zionist Federation.

▲ The Balfour Declaration,
signed by Arthur James
Balfour, foreign secretary
of the U.K., 1917
Granger Historical Picture Archive /
British Museum

▲▶ King Faisal (*front*) posing
with guests at his party,
including T.E. Lawrence
(*third from right*),
during the Paris Peace
Conference, 1919
Wikimedia Commons

was the Arab state promised during the war; others, however, felt that the Arabs had been betrayed.

The transition from Ottoman to European control of the colonial territories had a profound impact on the Sephardi Jews who lived in Arab lands after the war. Although most of the Sephardi were still living in their ancestral homelands, they were now controlled by the major European powers. France had Morocco (which they took in 1912), Algeria, Tunisia, Lebanon, and much of Syria; Italy had Libya; and Britain had Egypt, Iraq, the port of Aden, and the mandate in Palestine.

The colonial powers were broadly friendlier to Jewish rights than their Muslim predecessors had been. From the point of view of the Arabs, however, they were a complete disaster, particularly the British—who had not only betrayed Arab national ambitions, but had also given away Palestine to the Jews.

This complex cauldron of colonialism, thwarted Arab national ambitions, Zionism, Jewish resentment of their ongoing *dhimmi* status, and the traditional Muslim view of Jews as second-class citizens created a challenging environment for the Sephardi. The emergence of the Nazis in the early 1930s, with their powerful anti-Semitic propaganda machine, compounded the situation. The response to these forces in the interwar years varied from country to country, and with it the situation of the Jews.

"My best friend was a
Muslim from an Egyptian
aristocratic family.
They lived in the palace
across the street."

EGYPT

During the interwar period, Egypt was a reasonably good place to be Jewish. Although the Jews did not enjoy citizenship, they were allowed to lead their lives largely unmolested. There were more than 80,000 of them and sixty synagogues scattered throughout the country, with the greatest concentration in Cairo and Alexandria.

Levana Vidal Zamir (above) was born in Cairo in 1938. Parts of her family had been in Egypt for 2,000 years. Her father was a wealthy man, who owned a printing business that had extensive contracts with the Egyptian Ministry of Education. Her life as a young girl, as she describes it, was idyllic. As she told Sephardi Voices, they lived in "a villa with a lot of rooms, bedrooms, and a very large garden, with jasmine and benches all around . . . my best friend was a Muslim from an Egyptian aristocratic family. They lived in the palace across the street."[4]

At the highest levels of society, relations with the Egyptian government were very good. Jews were even members of the cabinet. In 1926, financier Joseph Cattaui Pasha became the minister of finance. The prime minister would show up every year at the Ben Ezra Synagogue in Cairo for the Kol Nidrei prayer that took place at the start of the Day of Atonement (Yom Kippur). In a similar way, when influential members of the Jewish community died, the government would send its most senior officials to the funerals. At the funeral for Joseph Cattaui Pasha, the prime minister and two former prime ministers showed up. The governor of Alexandria read the eulogy.

At the same time, other developments were laying the seeds for future problems. In 1928, Hassan al-Banna created the Muslim Brotherhood. Its target was not just Zionism, but to stir up hatred against the Jews as well. Its very first topic for debate was "The Subject of Palestine and the Necessity of Jihad."

The ascension of Adolf Hitler to power added to the waves of anti-Semitism. Beginning in the mid-1930s, the Nazis began broadcasting hatred of Jews to all the Muslim countries of the Middle East. A key line of attack was to remind everyone that the British had sided with the Jews against the Arabs when they endorsed the Balfour Declaration's commitment to a Jewish homeland in Palestine.

▲▲ Levana Zamir (*front row, fifth from left*) and her Hebrew class, which includes five of her six brothers, at the Talmud Torah school in Helwan, Egypt, 1947. The two adults in the center are Joseph Azouli, the administrator of the school, and Esther Azouli, the Hebrew teacher and his wife. Joseph was later arrested at the same time as 1,400 other Jewish men in Cairo and Alexandria. After a year and a half in prison without trial, he was released and expelled from Egypt. He died shortly thereafter.
Courtesy of Levana Zamir

▲ Ezra Zamir-Belbel (*right*), Levana Zamir's future husband, poses with his friends (one is Jewish, one Christian, and one Muslim) in Giza, Egypt, 1945.
Courtesy of Levana Zamir

▶ Hassan al-Banna (1906–1949), founder of the Muslim Brotherhood
Chronicle of World History / Alamy Stock Photo

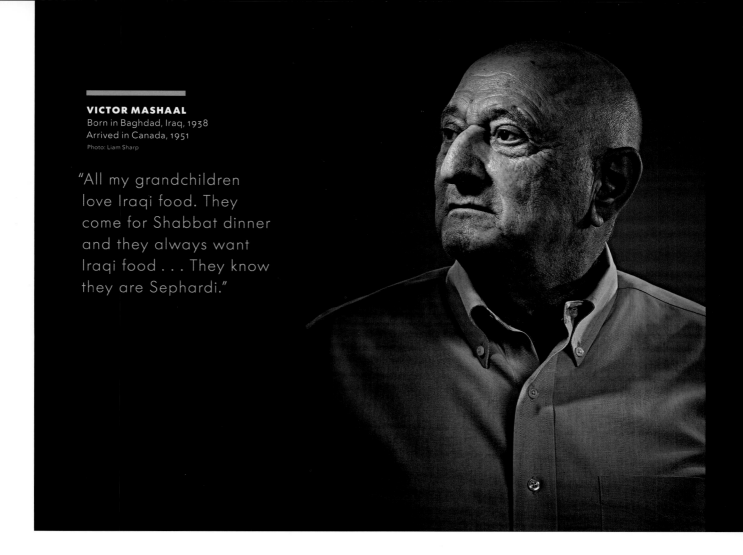

VICTOR MASHAAL
Born in Baghdad, Iraq, 1938
Arrived in Canada, 1951
Photo: Liam Sharp

"All my grandchildren love Iraqi food. They come for Shabbat dinner and they always want Iraqi food . . . They know they are Sephardi."

IRAQ

When the British conquered Baghdad in 1917, they were welcomed by the Jews (the Babylonian Jews) as liberators from the yoke of *dhimmi* status under the Turks. Full citizenship was extended to the local Jews, who flourished despite ongoing harassment. By the end of the 1930s, there were close to 135,000 Jews in Iraq. They comprised much of Iraq's industrial, commercial, and financial sectors. They were central to its economic growth and prosperity, and became integrated in the social, political, and cultural life of the country.

Many of them lived very comfortable lives. Victor Mashaal (above), for example, grew up in a wealthy family. His father was "the distributor for Firestone tires, Harvester trucks, Rolls Royce machinery, and other world class companies. He was not a Zionist, but he identified with the Jews, helped Jewish people to do whatever, sending parts to Israel [Palestine]." They lived in a large house with servants and gardens, and were highly integrated members of the Iraqi upper class.

► Baghdad Chamber of Commerce, 1938. Meir Basri (*standing, far left*), a grandson of Chief Rabbi Hakham Ezra Dangoor, was a leader in the Iraqi Jewish Community, the co-founder of the chamber of commerce, and for many years its secretary-general. Mohammed Kamel Al Khederi (*sitting, back right*) was the secretary, and Ibrahim Haim Moallem Itzhak (*sitting, back left*) its deputy director.
Courtesy of Aida Zelouf

► King Faisal (*front row, center*) visits the Laura Kadoorie Alliance School for Girls, Baghdad, including Chief Rabbi Hakham Ezra Dangoor (*front row, in black robes*) in 1924.
Courtesy of Aida Zelouf

"At the races my father
with his Muslim friends
sat in his box next to
the king's box."

Lisette Shashoua Ades (above) remembers an idyllic Baghdad. "I had a lovely childhood. Our house was right on the Tigris River, so you could hear the rippling of water at night and see the stars and the moon. My dad had racehorses, Arab stallions. His partner was a Muslim. And at the races my father with his Muslim friends sat in his box next to the king's box."

Ezra Zilkha (page 28) also was born into a wealthy Baghdad family. His father established the famous Zilkha Bank and a multigenerational financial dynasty.

I am a Baghdad Jew. My father was a banker. He started his bank in 1899. In 1902, he went to Istanbul. He traveled first by caravan to Aleppo and then by train to Istanbul. He opened a branch in Beirut in 1927, in Damascus in 1935, in Cairo in 1937, and in Alexandria in 1939. My father would take me out of school to go on trips with him. I went to Palestine in the 1930s. In 1931, my father bought the Anglo-Palestine Bank, now Bank Leumi. We traveled by car

EZRA ZILKHA
Born in Baghdad, Iraq, 1925
Arrived in the United States, 1951
Photo: Liam Sharp

"My native language is Arabic . . . I speak Baghdad Arabic."

from Beirut to Haifa and Tel Aviv. Tel Aviv was a modern city; Haifa was an Arab city. My connection was more to Arabic culture than Jewish. I was more comfortable with the Arabs than the Jewish Palestinians.

In fact, as he noted later in life: "I'm a Jew, an Arab Jew. My native language is Arabic. That means I speak Baghdad Arabic, that I remember the stories of Baghdad. I feel it very strongly when I'm with my Arab friends. I'm very much at home. I feel very proud of what I am."

The Zilkha Bank group would become one of the biggest financial groups in the Middle East and North Africa.

Almost two-thirds of the Jews in Iraq lived in Baghdad, which was the spiritual center for all Jews living east of Damascus. Not all, however, were wealthy bankers and friends of the king. Many lived very modestly and sometimes in significant poverty. The Kurdish Jews of Mosul were less integrated, and their situation with their Muslim neighbors was often very difficult.

Like the Jews of Egypt, the situation of the Babylonian Jews (Iraqi Jews) was often perilous. It became worse after Hitler came to power, validating anti-Semitism and appealing to Iraq's sense of grievance against the U.K. In the 1940s, this would plunge the Iraqi Jewish community into a full-blown crisis.

MOROCCO

Like the Jews of Egypt and Iraq, the Jews of Morocco had been there since the time of the Second Temple. They consisted of urban and rural Jews, both those who had been there for as long as records were kept and those who had arrived from Spain and Portugal in the wake of the Inquisition. These Sephardi also included large numbers of villagers and mountain dwellers, who lived among the Amazigh (the Berbers).

With the conquest of Morocco by the French in 1912, the situation of the Jews improved considerably. *Dhimmi* status was ended and they increasingly went to French language schools, run by the Alliance Israélite Universelle, becoming Europeanized in a way that their Muslim neighbors did not, paralleling the circumstances of the Jews in Spanish Morocco.

Although the Jews were not granted full citizenship until 1956, the decades of the 1920s and '30s were a period of prosperity. They advanced in business, government, and the arts. By the 1940s, there were almost 250,000 Jews in Morocco. This made them the largest Jewish population in any Arab country.

The relative safety of Jewish life in Morocco was occasionally broken by outbreaks of anti-Jewish violence. Emile Wahnich (see page 32) was born in Fez in 1931. He recalls his parent's account of the pogrom in their city: "There was a lot

▲◀ Signage for the first branch of Zilkha Bank, founded in Baghdad in 1899
Courtesy of the Zilkha family

▲ *Left to right*: Ezra, Abdulla, Khedouri, Maurice, and Selim Zilkha, Cairo, 1946
Courtesy of the Zilkha family

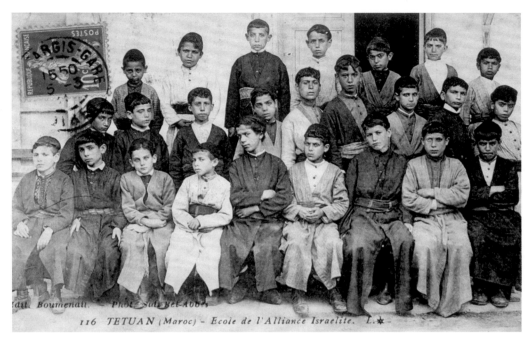

116 TETUAN (Maroc) - Ecole de l'Alliance Israelite. L.⋆

Bouhsira, photo-édit. - Fez
589. FEZ — Jeunes filles Israélites
déguisées pour fêter Jeanne-d'Arc

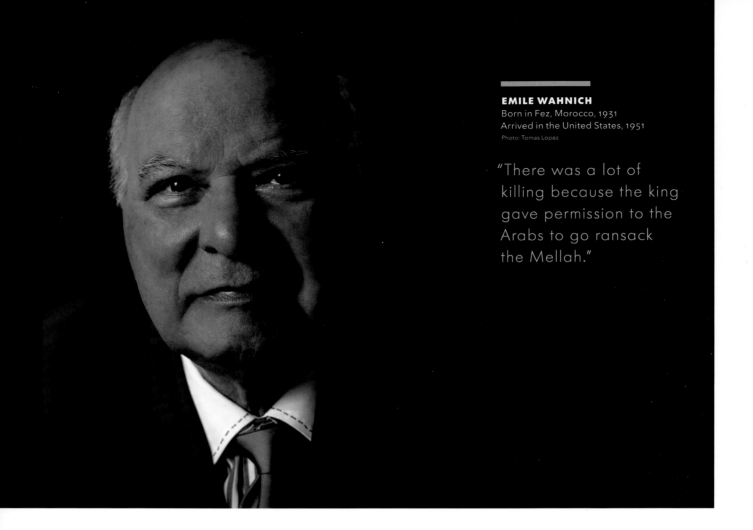

EMILE WAHNICH
Born in Fez, Morocco, 1931
Arrived in the United States, 1951
Photo: Tomas Lopez

"There was a lot of
killing because the king
gave permission to the
Arabs to go ransack
the Mellah."

Emile Wahnich (*center*)
at age four, with his cousin
Ninette Wahnich (*left*) and his
sister Simy Wahnich, Fez, 1935
Courtesy of Emile Wahnich

of killing because the king gave permission to the Arabs to go ransack the Mellah [the Jewish quarter]. It was very, very bad because a lot of lives were lost. A lot of people were hidden in the wells; they used to hide in them to save their lives."

He himself was subject to anti-Semitic attacks as a child. "One time, I was a kid, I was coming home and suddenly a woman caught me ... and there were certainly hundreds of people surrounding me ... and she beat me up because, she said, I insulted her religion. [I said,] 'What religion? I don't know what religion it is'... The police came and took me ... to the police station. My father was called in. We had to settle with the woman. We had to give her money." Like all the Jews of Morocco, Wahnich lived in a double world: he was in a homeland he loved, but always in danger.

▼ The Crémieux Decree.
TRANSLATION: "Republic of
France No. 136—A decree
declaring the Jews native to
Algeria to be French citizens.

"The Government of National
Defense decrees: The Jews
native to French Algeria are
declared French citizens; as
a result, their status, both
real and personal, will be,
from the promulgation of
this decree, subject to the
laws of France, with all rights
acquired before this day
remaining intact.

"Any legislation, any Senate
advice, decrees, regulations,
or orders to the contrary are
abolished.

Made at Tours,
October 24, 1870."

ALGERIA AND TUNISIA

The French conquest of Algeria in 1830 had improved the situation of the local Jews significantly. In 1870, the Crémieux Decree granted French citizenship to Jews in the major coastal cities. The civil rights of the Jews in Algeria were the best in the Muslim world. At the same time, the Crémieux Decree made it very difficult for Muslims to qualify for French citizenship. Over time, this would drive an enormous wedge between the Jewish and Muslim Algerians.

The Algerian Jews experienced a rapid and rather extreme form of French acculturation. The presence of the Alliance Israélite Universelle school system allowed many Jews to provide their children with a French education, as it had in Morocco. Those who could afford it sent their sons to university in France.

By the late 1930s, there were more than 130,000 Jews in Algeria. Although they continued to speak Arabic, they were increasingly better educated, more French, and more European in outlook than their neighbors. This gave them significant advantages over the local Arabs, making it easier for them to prosper. They began to command better positions in

B. n° 8.　　　　— 109 —
RÉPUBLIQUE FRANÇAISE.

N° 136. — Décret qui déclare citoyens français les Israélites
indigènes de l'Algérie.
Du 24 Octobre 1870.

LE GOUVERNEMENT DE LA DÉFENSE NATIONALE
DÉCRÈTE :

Les israélites indigènes des départements de l'Algérie sont déclarés citoyens français; en conséquence, leur statut réel et leur statut personnel seront, à compter de la promulgation du présent décret, réglés par la loi française, tous droits acquis jusqu'à ce jour restant inviolables.
Toute disposition législative, tout sénatus-consulte, décret, règlement ou ordonnance contraires, sont abolis.
Fait à Tours, le 24 Octobre 1870.
Signé AD. CRÉMIEUX, L. GAMBETTA, AL. GLAIS-BIZOIN, L. FOURICHON.

RÉPUBLIQUE FRANÇAISE.

N° 137. — Décret sur la Naturalisation des Indigènes musulmans
et des Étrangers résidant en Algérie.
Du 24 Octobre 1870.

ALGER — 28. La Synagogue

Coll. spéciale D. G.

Deuxième Année. — N° 26   5 CENTIMES   Dimanche 4 Juin 1899

PRÉFECTURE D'ALGER
DÉPÔT LÉGAL

Supplément du Nouvel illustré Antijuif

L'Algérie aux Français !   RÉDACTION & ADMINISTRATION
Villa Antijuive, 34, Boulevard Bon-Accueil
Alger-Mustapha   A la Porte les Juifs !

LUTAUD OGRE

▲ The Great Synagogue
in Algiers, also known as
the Synagogue de
Rue Randon, c. 1921.
The synagogue was
ransacked in 1940.
Musée d'art et d'histoire du Judaïsme

▲▶ The cover of an 1899
supplement of *L'Antijuif
algérien*, an anti-
Semitic newspaper that
organized petitions and
demonstrations against
Jews and government
officials
Bibliothèque nationale de France

Algerian society. Many came to do well in business, education, and administration. Inevitably, this aggravated the historic anti-Semitism of the dominant Arab community.

Like Algeria and Morocco, Tunisia evolved as a French colony. In 1881, it became a French protectorate. *Dhimmi* status was ended and the lives of local Jews grew easier. Once again, the Jews increasingly came under the influence of French language and culture. Children were sent to French language schools and later to university in France. Like the other two French colonies, Algeria and Morocco, this increased the differences between the Jewish and Muslim populations. At the end of the period between the wars, there were roughly 55,000 Jews in Tunisia, half of whom lived in Tunis.

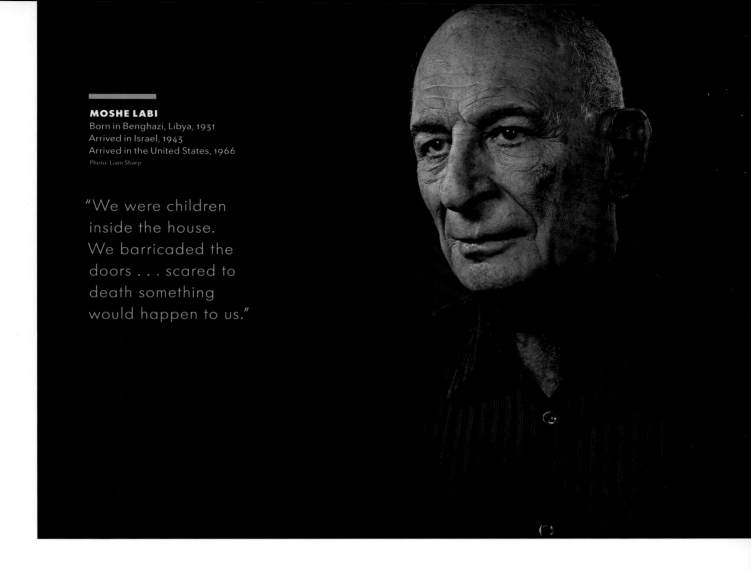

MOSHE LABI
Born in Benghazi, Libya, 1931
Arrived in Israel, 1943
Arrived in the United States, 1966
Photo: Liam Sharp

"We were children inside the house. We barricaded the doors . . . scared to death something would happen to us."

LIBYA

The population of Jews in Libya was the smallest of the North African countries in the 1930s, at only about 25,000. Two-thirds lived in Tripoli and many of the rest in Benghazi.

The Italians conquered Libya in 1911. As it had with other European powers elsewhere, their arrival marked a major improvement in the civil status of the Jews. Until the beginning of World War II, when Italy joined Germany as the two Axis powers, the Jews prospered and enjoyed reasonably good relations with their Muslim neighbors.

Moshe Labi (above) was born in Benghazi in 1931. He could trace his family back to 1500, in a long line of rabbis. He describes the Jewish position as being a "bridge" between the Italians and the Arabs. He spoke Judaeo-Arabic at home and Italian and Arabic in the street.

▲ Moshe Labi at age three (*right*), with his brother Aldo and their parents, Benghazi, Libya, 1934
Courtesy of Moshe Labi

▶ Passport of Ghita Labi, mother of Moshe Labi, 1936
Courtesy of Moshe Labi

Hamos Guetta was born in Tripoli in 1955. His grandfather was a rabbi and a pupil of the chief rabbi of Palestine. He too spoke Arabic, but was educated in Italian. He left Libya when he was twelve and moved to Italy, but his identity was deeply shaped by his family's roots: "My father and I were more Arab Jews than Italian Jews. Its [Tunisia's] smells and perfumes made you a Jew of that land. Your feet were colored by the Sahara desert and the warm soil of Libya and the palm trees surrounding you. I am not 100 percent Italian. I am no longer Libyan, but perhaps more Libyan than Italian."

SYRIA

Like in Libya, the Jewish community in Syria was small. Joseph Abouti was born into an upper-class neighbourhood there in the 1930s. "There was a lot of trust between the Arabs and the Jews in those days," he says. "My father had a lot of good friends, the mayor and judges in Aleppo. He played cards every day with them. The coffeehouse was at the corner and I would go and see him. Sometimes there was a very bad pogrom. The mayor took my family to his house to protect them."

Despite his family's strong political and social connections, he yearned to go to Palestine and fight for a Jewish state. And he was very determined: "I stole money from my father's pocket and I bought a ticket to Beirut. I wanted to cross the border illegally into Palestine and join the underground. My father caught me and said, 'Son, you are too young. Stay. Continue your education. After that you can go.' I listened, then tried again. Stole money and he caught me again. The third time, he arranged for me to go with some other people to Beirut and from there I went to Palestine."

PALESTINE

Of all the lands in the Middle East, the most vexed was Palestine. The Jews and the local Arabs had different views about its future. Inspired by Zionism, Jews had been buying land and settling there since the late nineteenth century. For their part, the local Arab population thought that it should be part of an independent Arab state.

Stereograph of a mason at a building site in Tel Aviv, 1920s

G. Eric and Edith Matson Photograph Collection, Prints and Photographs Collection, Library of Congress, LC-M32-B-448

▲ Jewish families flee
  Jerusalem's Old City
  at the Jaffa Gate,
  August 1929.

▶ British troops march
  through Jerusalem in a
  display of force intended
  to quell riots, August 1929.

▲ In Jaffa, a series of violent
anti-Jewish riots in April
1936 left fourteen Jewish
people and two non-
Jewish Arabs dead.
Courtesy of the Central Zionist Archives

◄ A desecrated synagogue
after riots in Hebron
Courtesy of the Central Zionist Archives

The confusion over Palestine's future was compounded when the British effectively occupied it during World War I and then had it handed to them as a protectorate by the Paris Peace Conference of 1919. The local Arab population was angered by British occupation, since it believed that the British had promised the Arabs a different outcome.

The Mufti of Jerusalem stoked the Palestinians' sense of anger and betrayal when he claimed that the Jewish settlers had designs on the Muslim holy places in Jerusalem. In 1929, riots broke out. In Jerusalem, forty Jews were killed and 4,000 fled their homes. In Hebron, more than sixty Jews were killed.

In 1936, riots began again as a protest against British rule. The principal demand was a halt to Jewish immigration to Palestine. This was widely supported by all the Muslim governments. By the end of the turmoil, eighty Jews had been killed, thirty-three British soldiers and more than 140 Arabs. By the end of the 1930s there were 940,000 Arabs and 370,000 Jews in Palestine, and the situation had become very tense. Both populations ultimately came to despise not just each other, but the British occupying forces as well.

Yemeni immigrants to
Palestine during the Fourth
Aliyah (the fourth major
wave of immigration to
Palestine), 1929
Courtesy of the Central Zionist Archives

YEMEN

The Jews of Yemen were also a very old community that had, like many of the others, been there since the beginning of time. In the nineteenth century, they had been much persecuted and discriminated against. They were not allowed to ride horses, had to wear special clothes, and could not build houses bigger than their Muslim neighbors had.

The situation in Yemen between the wars was, if anything, even more difficult. A particularly rigorous understanding of *dhimmi* status prevailed. The most egregious example was the forced conversion of Jewish orphans. In 1922, a new decree was issued, requiring the police to search out and arrest orphans—"orphans" being any Jewish child that did not have a father. The children were taken from their mothers, imprisoned, and, through a combination of punishments and bribes, made to accept Islam.

By the end of the 1930s, there were about 50,000 Jews in Yemen. The only ones who weren't cruelly treated were those in Aden, which was under the control of the British.

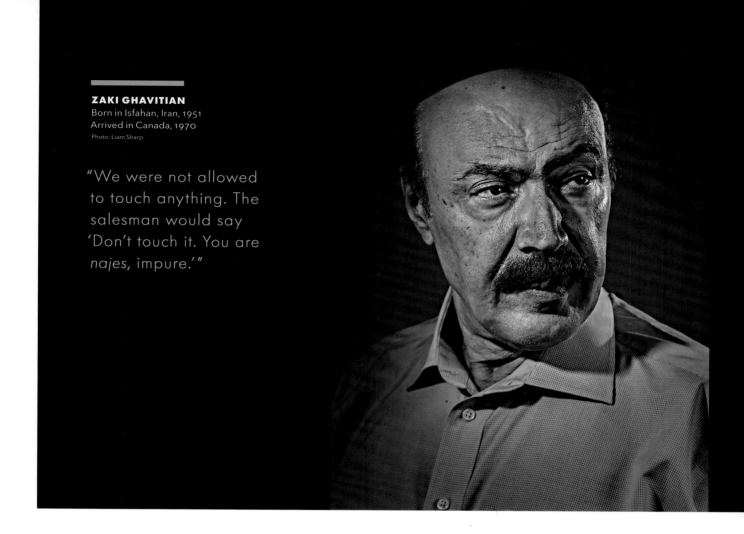

"We were not allowed to touch anything. The salesman would say 'Don't touch it. You are *najes*, impure.'"

IRAN

The Persian Jews were among the oldest Jewish communities in the Fertile Crescent. They, too, like the Babylonian Jews, had been in their ancestral home since the beginning of recorded history. Although not considered Arab Jews, since they spoke Farsi, the Jews of Iran constituted a sizeable population. By the late 1940s, there were roughly 90,000 of them.

Their legal situation conformed to the traditional Muslim *dhimmi* status. For hundreds of years they had lived under a Shia theocracy that forced them to pay the jizya tax and emphasized their uncleanliness. This changed dramatically in 1926, when the shah took power and abolished the jizya, granting all subjects equal rights.

Despite their new status, the Jews continued to suffer from anti-Semitism. Zaki Ghavitian (above) describes its effects:

> My great-grandparents are from Kashan, not far from Isfahan, the city of my birth. My grandmother and mother both wore traditional dress, the chador.

Near my village was another village in which the Jews were forcibly converted.

They knew my grandfather was Jewish because he had a beard and every time they passed him on the small alley, they would take his cap and pull his beard. I hid under his coat. One day, I went shopping with him in the market for fruit. We were not allowed to touch anything. The salesman would say "Don't touch it. You are *najes*, impure."

In Tehran and the larger cities, however, the shah's new laws allowed many Jews to prosper and become deeply integrated into the country's social and cultural life. This would last until the shah was overthrown by Ayatollah Khomeini and Iran reverted to a Shia theocracy in 1979.

The Zargar family, including Shahverdi Zargar (*seated, center*), jeweler to the king of Persia, Turkmenistan, c. 1908
Courtesy of Lina Samimy

THE SEPHARDI DURING WORLD WAR II

By the end of the 1930s, as war broke out again in Europe, there were over 800,000 Jews in Arab lands and Iran, not counting the 370,000 in Palestine. Their situations varied dramatically. In some countries they were treated reasonably well; in other countries very badly. In all cases, there were dark underlying tensions that would erupt in a full-blown catastrophe after the war.

At the beginning of World War II, the Nazis enjoyed extraordinary military victories, defeating France in a matter of weeks and installing a puppet government at Vichy. With that, the French colonies in North Africa, in the Maghreb—Morocco, Algeria, and Tunisia—fell under the sway of Germany's ferociously anti-Semitic policies.

The Nazis' propaganda broadcasts to the Arab world escalated in frequency and intensity. They played them not only to incite disdain for Jews in Muslim communities, but to make the point over and over again that Britain was an imperial power occupying one of the Arab homelands, Palestine, and that Germany believed in Arab independence.

Many of the leading Muslim officials—including the Mufti of Jerusalem and Rashid Ali, the prime minister of Iraq—were fascists who supported the Nazis' ambitions unreservedly. Other Muslim leaders, while not overtly fascist, resented the Balfour Declaration, the British occupation of Palestine, and the United Kingdom's support of Zionism.

This complex set of forces triggered different responses in the various Arab countries. The extension of Vichy France's control over the French colonies

resulted in the passage of anti-Jewish regulations and the legitimization of pogroms and violence.

In 1940 and 1941, anti-Semitic rioting broke out in Tunisia. Similar events occurred in Morocco and Algeria. In many cases, the local governments were afraid to intervene to protect Jews for fear of displeasing their Muslim citizens and the Vichy government.

▲ A Muslim mob
breaks into the Great
Synagogue (the
Synagogue de Rue
Randon, see also
page 34), in Algiers,
c. 1940.
Courtesy of the Central
Zionist Archives

◄ Jewish men, forced
into labor by German
soldiers, march with
spades while under
guard, Tunis, Tunisia,
1942.
Bundesarchiv, Bild 183-J20382

▶ Channah Sitbon with her
father Mordechai, Tunis,
Tunisia, 1939
Courtesy of Channah Ankri Sitbon

"My father stopped believing in Judaism when he became a prisoner of the Germans during the war."

Channah Ankri Sitbon (above) described the situation in Tunis when the Germans arrived: "They took all the men and put them in jail and left the wives and children alone. They tortured them. They hung my dad from a tree and whipped him. After the war ended, he came home filthy and full of lice. My father stopped believing in Judaism when he became a prisoner of the Germans during the war."

In other cases, Jews were rounded up and forced into labor camps. The same thing happened in Libya after the Italians, with German help, drove out the British. Moshe Labi recalls the terrors associated with the German arrival: "There was a pogrom in Benghazi taking place in the streets. We were children inside the house. We barricaded the doors; we were scared to death that something would happen to us. My father was taken to the concentration camp. We were suffering from malnutrition. The ration was half a loaf of bread per person per day."

As the war wore on, they were subject to constant bombardment. "Over a year, every night, bombs fell," says Labi. "When I hear people talking about PTSD, I say to myself, I went through that . . . The first time I realized it was deep in my head was when 9/11 happened. I was in Texas, watching what was happening to

the Twin Towers, and all of a sudden, I was very sick, feeling like I was there. And for the rest of the day, I was literally physically sick."

The planned deportation of the Jews and the arrival of mobile gas chambers in Libya were averted only when the Allied forces routed the Axis in North Africa in 1943.

Even as these events were occurring, important political figures in Tunisia, Algeria, and Morocco attempted to extend protection to their Jewish communities. The bey of Tunis, Moncef Bey (effectively the king), summoned his senior officials when the Germans occupied Tunisia and said: "The Jews are having a hard time but they are under our patronage and we are responsible for their lives. If I find out an Arab informer caused even one hair of a Jew to fall, this Arab will pay with his life."[5]

King Mohammed V of Morocco famously met with the representatives of Nazi Germany and Vichy France and told them that in his country there were no Muslim citizens and no Jewish citizens, there were only Moroccan citizens. No Jews were deported from Morocco to concentration camps in Europe.

In a similar way, when Sheik Taieb el-Okbi heard rumors in Algeria that plans were being made to launch pogroms, he immediately issued a formal prohibition on Muslims attacking Jews. When Jewish goods were seized by the Vichy authorities, he wrote an instruction to the mosques saying: "Our brothers are suffering misfortune. Do not take their goods." Not one Arab agreed to be an administrator of confiscated Jewish property.[6]

This complex and sometimes contradictory set of circumstances kept the Jews of North Africa relatively safe, in comparison with the atrocities committed in Europe. There were no government-sponsored mass killings as there were at camps like Auschwitz and Treblinka in German-occupied Poland.

In Iraq, however, the situation was very different. Rashid Ali al-Gaylani, a former prime minister, spurred on by the Germans and Italians, engineered a revolt against the moderate pro-British government of Nuri Said. On taking power in the spring of 1941, he restored relations with the Nazis and appointed Yunis al-Sabawi, who translated *Mein Kampf* into Arabic, as minister of finance.

Later that year, the Mufti of Jerusalem, fearing arrest by the British in Palestine, moved to Baghdad with many of his anti-Semitic followers. In May, attacks on Jews began throughout Baghdad. The followers of the Mufti, pro-Nazi students, demobilized soldiers and off-duty policemen, and the Katayib al-Shabab militia began the most fearsome pogrom in modern Iraq's history.

The attacks came to be known as the Farhud (the "violent dispossession"). They resulted in almost 200 Jews killed,

▲▲ Protesters carry flags and wave swords during a demonstration in central Baghdad, 1935. There is no known image of the Farhud, but it may have looked something like this.
Otheniel Margalit Collection, Yad Izhak Ben-Zvi

▲ Rashid Ali al-Gaylani, the former prime minister of Iraq who in 1941 instigated a revolt against British influence in his country, speaks in Berlin with fellow countrymen and the Mufti of Jerusalem (*front row, left*), 1943.
Sueddeutsche Zeitung Photo / Alamy Stock Photo

SAMI SOURANI
Born in Baghdad, Iraq, 1934
Arrived in Israel, 1950
Arrived in Canada, 1961
Photo: Liam Sharp

"You can hear the voice of the people asking for mercy . . . please don't kill us, please don't kill us."

2,000 wounded, and hundreds of women and girls raped. Over 900 houses, 600 shops, and four synagogues were looted.

Sami Sourani (above), who was born in Baghdad in 1934, describes the Farhud as he experienced it as an eight-year-old boy: "It was the first day of Shavuot, and all the houses of the Jews were marked with a sign that this is a house of the Jews. And they attacked, breaking into houses, killing the people and taking money. You can hear, at night you can hear the voice of the people asking for mercy, you know, please don't kill us, please don't kill us. It was not far from us and we were afraid. We didn't know what to do."

Abdullah Dangoor, who was born in Baghdad twenty years earlier than Sami Sourani, also lived through the Farhud. As he describes it, "The Arabs attacked the Jewish quarter, or rather the Jewish quarters . . . Jews were living together and everybody knew which houses they wanted to attack . . . and property they wanted to steal. It ended after two days, but it remained in the mind of all Jews . . . The things we never experienced before."

There is a tone of betrayal in his account. It is not just the horror of the pogrom that disturbs him, it is also the sense of abandonment by his neighbors and his country. The Jews of Baghdad were highly integrated into Iraqi society. When they went to school, Dangoor says, "All the subjects were studied in Arabic. Mathematics, physics, and everything else was in Arabic."

Jews were central to the city's cultural, social, and commercial life. They often thought of themselves as Iraqi first and Jewish second. And why not? As Dangoor notes, even after escaping Iraq in 1948 and living in the United Kingdom for decades, "Definitely, I am not British. But how can I deny that I am an Iraqi? I didn't go there as an immigrant. We have been there for 3,000 years." This is a point that he would make directly to his Muslim friends. He would tell them, "It was our country… we were here before you. We have more right than you have."

And yet, 3,000 years was not enough to claim full citizenship, not enough to protect the oldest residents of Babylon from persecution, not enough to save them from "the things we never experienced before."

▲ Abdullah Dangoor (*left*) with brother Naim, London, 1934
Courtesy of David Dangoor

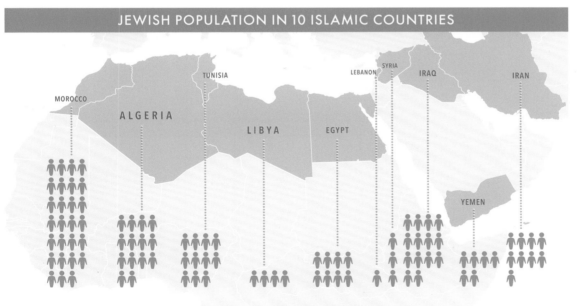

JEWISH POPULATION IN 10 ISLAMIC COUNTRIES

1948: 946,000

Source: sephardivoices.com

THE EXODUS BEGINS: 1948–1967

"For a week, we didn't know whether my brother was dead or alive."

MARIA MEGHNAGI ARON

3 **AS WORLD WAR II** wound down, ongoing tensions among the advocates of Arab nationalism and Zionism boiled over. Pogroms escalated across the Jewish Arab world. Hundreds of Jews were killed and injured, houses and synagogues looted and destroyed. In Libya alone, an estimated 4,200 Jewish traders and artisans were made destitute.

Violet-Albertine Shohet and her three boys on the Al-Karkh, the left shore of the Tigris River, Baghdad, Iraq, October 1957, a year before the overthrow of the Iraqi monarchy
Courtesy of David Shohet

In March 1945, Syria, Iraq, Egypt, Lebanon, Yemen, Saudi Arabia, and Jordan formed the Arab League. Its purpose was to coordinate the political aims of its members, particularly their resistance to the creation of a Jewish state in Palestine. As part of its work, the league organized an international criminal conspiracy to deny Jews living in Islamic lands their rights. It took the form of a legal framework, drafted by the political committee of the Arab League, that resembled the Nuremberg Laws of Nazi Germany. It defined all Jews as Zionists and therefore enemies of the state. Jewish property was to be sequestered, bank accounts frozen, assets seized, and citizenship denied.

▲ Representatives of seven Arab states meet in Cairo, Egypt, on May 29, 1946. Kings, presidents, and princes convened at the invitation of King Farouk to organize a united front against Jewish immigration to Palestine.
AP Photo

▲▶ Arab students of the American University in Cairo carry a banner advocating for an Arab Palestine on December 2, 1947. They joined Egyptians demonstrating in Cairo against Palestine's partition.
AP Photo

▶ Moshe Sharet, Abba Eban, and David Hacohen (*touching the flag, left to right*) celebrate the United Nations' proclamation of the independence of the State of Israel, New York, 1947.
Government Press Office (Israel)

In November of 1947, the UN took up the debate on the future of Palestine. The Iraqi and Egyptian delegates forcefully made the point that Palestine belonged to the Arabs living there. They warned that there were almost a million Jews living in Arab countries and that the partition of Palestine "might create in these countries anti-Semitism even more difficult to root out than the anti-Semitism the Allies were trying to eradicate in Germany... [and could lead to] the massacre of a large number of Jews."[7]

After five days of debate, the UN adopted Resolution 181, calling for the partition of Palestine into two states, one Jewish and one Arab. The Arab world reacted with anger and alarm. The Palestinian Arabs, supported by the Arab League, rejected their own statehood and demanded sovereignty over all of British-mandated Palestine.

The proclamation of the creation of the State of Israel resonated profoundly throughout the Jewish communities in North Africa and the Middle East. More riots and pogroms quickly followed. In Aden, a British protectorate, the UN vote triggered violence that continued over a period of four days, killing more than eighty Jews and destroying hundreds of homes and shops.

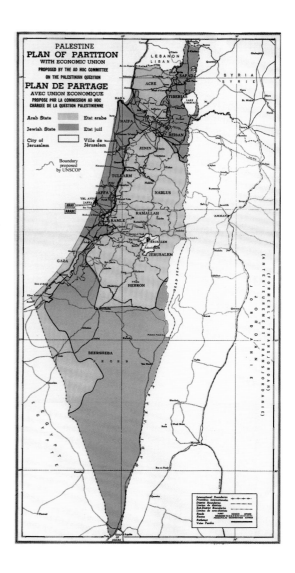

▶ Map showing the partition of Palestine proposed in November 1947 by the United Nations Ad Hoc Committee, with the earlier (September 1947) proposal by the UN Special Committee on Palestine in green. The plan was adopted by the UN on November 29, but it immediately caused civil war to break out in Palestine, and the plan was not implemented.
United Nations Cartographic Section / Wikimedia Commons

◀ The el-Keslassy family celebrates the founding of the State of Israel on the occasion of Haim's (*middle center*) bar mitzvah, Fez, Morocco, 1948.
Courtesy of David Cohen

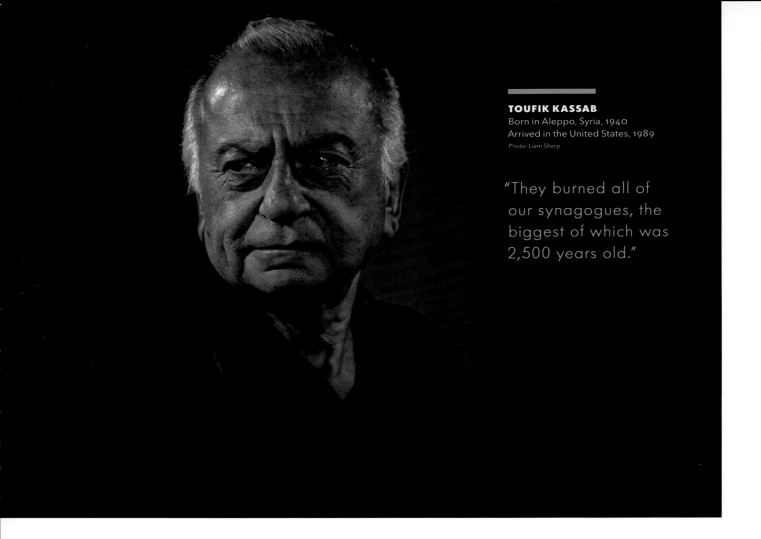

"They burned all of our synagogues, the biggest of which was 2,500 years old."

Toufik Kassab, Aleppo, Syria, 1946
Courtesy of Toufik Kassab

In Syria, all eighteen synagogues in Aleppo were ruined and as many as 6,000 of the 7,000 Jewish inhabitants fled the city. Toufik Kassab (above), only a child of seven at the time, recalls the terror: "In 1947, when Israel received the UN vote, all the Arab people in Aleppo were against the Jews. So they started to go behind the Jews. They burned all of our synagogues, the biggest of which was 2,500 years old." The same thing happened in Cairo, where a mob once again attacked the Jewish quarter.

The Arab League met in Cairo in early 1948 and approved a plan for economic, political, and military measures to be taken in response to the Palestinian crisis. As part of these measures, the members of the league agreed to implement in each of their countries the legal framework created by the political committee. The Jews in Arab lands would then effectively be declared enemies of their respective states and lose all property and assets.

THE PALESTINE POST

If you can't come to town, please telephone **4607**

Lighting, Heating, Cooking, Refrigeration

CARL MARX
3 PRINCESS MARY AVE., JERUSALEM

JERUSALEM
SUNDAY, MAY 16, 1948

PRICE: 25 MILS
VOL. XXIII. No. 6714

THE PALESTINE POST
THE SUBSCRIPTION DEPARTMENT has returned to The Palestine Post offices, Hasolel Street, Jerusalem, Tel. 4233.

STATE OF ISRAEL IS BORN

The first independent Jewish State in 19 centuries was born in Tel Aviv as the British Mandate over Palestine came to an end at midnight on Friday, and it was immediately subjected to the test of fire. As "Medinat Yisrael" (State of Israel) was proclaimed, the battle for Jerusalem raged, with most of the city falling to the Jews. At the same time, President Truman announced that the United States would accord recognition to the new State. A few hours later, Palestine was invaded by Moslem armies from the south, east and north, and Tel Aviv was raided from the air. On Friday the United Nations Special Assembly adjourned after adopting a resolution to appoint a mediator but without taking any action on the Partition Resolution of November 29.

Yesterday the battle for the Jerusalem-Tel Aviv road was still under way, and two Arab villages were taken. In the north, Acre town was captured, and the Jewish Army consolidated its positions in Western Galilee.

THE WAR OF INDEPENDENCE

On May 14, 1948, Israel declared independence. Two days later, it was attacked by the armies of the Arab League.

Egypt, Syria, Lebanon, Jordan, and Iraq moved simultaneously to snuff out the newly created Jewish state. The fighting was intense. By June, Egyptian troops had advanced as far as the southern suburbs of Jerusalem and Iraqi forces were within sight of the Mediterranean. Yet the Jews were not—as the Arabs predicted—driven into the sea. They fought on.

The war led Arab governments to increase the pressure on their Jewish citizens. In Egypt, the prime minister declared a state of emergency and plans to arrest all Communists. The declaration asserted that all Jews were Zionists and all Zionists were Communists. Hundreds of Jews were arrested and their property sequestered. Those that were not arrested were blocked from leaving Egypt.

In Iraq, similar measures were pursued. Jews were arrested and charged with giving support to Israel, including the richest Jew, Shafiq Ades, who had lunched with cabinet ministers and dined with the regent. He was put on trial, denied a defense, fined, and sentenced to death. He was hanged in public in front of his mansion in Basra. Nobody was safe.

In July, as the Arab offensive stalled and the realization dawned that the Jewish state might survive, anti-Israel and anti-Jewish feeling grew stronger. In Libya, mobs attacked the Jewish quarter in Tripoli, killing and looting. Similar outrages occurred in Egypt, where bombs were thrown, injuring and murdering more than sixty people. In Iraq, Zionist affiliation was made a criminal offense, all Jews in official positions were dismissed, and Jews were forbidden from leaving the country.

The situation was less dire in some countries than others. The king of Morocco called for calm and asked his subjects not to attack the Moroccan Jews, distinguishing them from the "rootless" Jews attempting to seize

▲ Front page of the *Palestine Post*, May 16, 1948
John Frost Newspapers / Alamy Stock Photo

▼ In the summer of 1948, Shafiq Ades, a wealthy Jewish Iraqi businessman, was accused of selling arms to Israel and of being a Communist. He was convicted without evidence by a military tribunal and hanged in front of a large crowd in September 1948.
Courtesy of Shlomo Hillel

▲ A mother and her family flee from square block of buildings in the Jewish district of Jerusalem, which were blasted to rubble in February 1948 before Israel took control of West Jerusalem in the War of Independence.
Everett Collection Inc / Alamy Stock Photo

▶ Barbed wire covers Princess Mary Avenue in Jerusalem at Zion Square to prevent counter-attacks after the War of Independence.
AP Photo

◄ Arab villagers, fleeing their homes during fighting in Galilee, stream out of Palestine on the road to Lebanon, November 4, 1948.
Photo: Jim Pringle / AP Photo

▼ An Israeli soldier questions Arab residents after curfew in Nazareth, July 17, 1948.
AP Photo

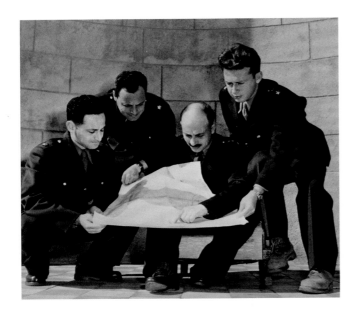

Palestine. In Iran, too, the shah refused to adopt a violent anti-Zionist stance. The Jews, in fact, were allowed to participate fully in the economic and social life of the country.

As the war ground on, Palestinian Arabs left their houses and villages. Some were pushed out by the Jewish forces; others simply fled to safety to avoid the fighting. Still others, encouraged by the Arab League, took flight of their own accord. Roughly 725,000 Palestinians became refugees, losing forever their houses and properties in what become known as the Nakba (Arabic for "catastrophe").

In November 1948, the Israeli army managed to push back the Arab forces, with the War of Independence (also known as the First Arab-Israeli War) ending in 1949. Armistice agreements were signed with Lebanon, Jordan, Egypt, and Syria. Only Iraq refused to sign, but withdrew its forces in March.

OPERATION MAGIC CARPET

The end of the war did not improve the situation of the Jews in Arab lands. To the contrary, they now understood that they would never be seen as Egyptians, Iraqis, or Libyans; they would always be seen as Zionists, fifth columnists and enemies of the countries where they had lived for hundreds and, in some cases, thousands of years.

Instead of a new beginning, the end of the war marked the beginning of the end of Jewish life in Ishmael's house. The great uprooting and emigration began in 1949 with the Jews leaving their ancient homelands. Some fled, some were expelled, and some were coerced into departing when their property and citizenship were confiscated.

In Yemen an extraordinary effort was made to airlift Jews out of the country. An Israeli-organized emigration, code-named Magic Carpet, was conducted entirely by air. None of those who left Yemen had ever flown before.

Mary Judah-Jacob Josielewski (page 60) was born in Aden in 1936. She lived in a small community of 5,000 Jews on five streets. No Muslims ever came to her house, except to see her father on business, and they were not allowed in the same room. The common language was Arabic, but there were two Arabics: the one spoken by the Muslims, and the one spoken by the Jews, which she describes as "like Arabic Yiddish because it's with Hebrew words and some Indian words and English words." It was dangerous to be heard speaking Jewish Arabic on the streets of Aden.

▲ Yemeni Jews arrive at Lod
Airport (now called Ben
Gurion Airport), 1950.
The Israeli government
organized Operation
Magic Carpet to airlift
Jews out of Yemen, where
they faced increasing
persecution.
Photo: Fritz Cohen / Government Press
Office (Israel)

◄ Yemeni Jews at an
immigrant camp near
Ein Shemer, Israel, 1950
Photo: Hans Pinn / Government Press
Office (Israel)

MARY JUDAH-JACOB JOSIELEWSKI
Born in Aden, Yemen, 1936
Arrived in Israel, 1949
Arrived in the United States, 1963
Photo: Michael Chavez

"A young guy, he was running with a baby in his arms. So they shot him [and the baby]."

Josielewski recalls the desperate situation of the Jews in Aden. She was only eleven when much of her family was killed. "My brother went to the roof and they shot him ... And so she [my mother] opened the window and said, 'Why did you kill my son?' So they shot her too. Almost in every family... someone died. A young guy, he was running with a baby in his arms. So they shot him [and the baby]."

At the age of twelve she left Yemen with her aunt and grandmother on the Magic Carpet. She could take only one bag, so she packed her "Shabbat dress and holiday dress and my beautiful shoes from India." She was not allowed to take any photographs, not even one of her mother.

Yitzhak Katab fled Yemen with his family when he was a young boy, first to Guela Camp outside Aden, and after several years on to Israel. He recalls life in Aden:

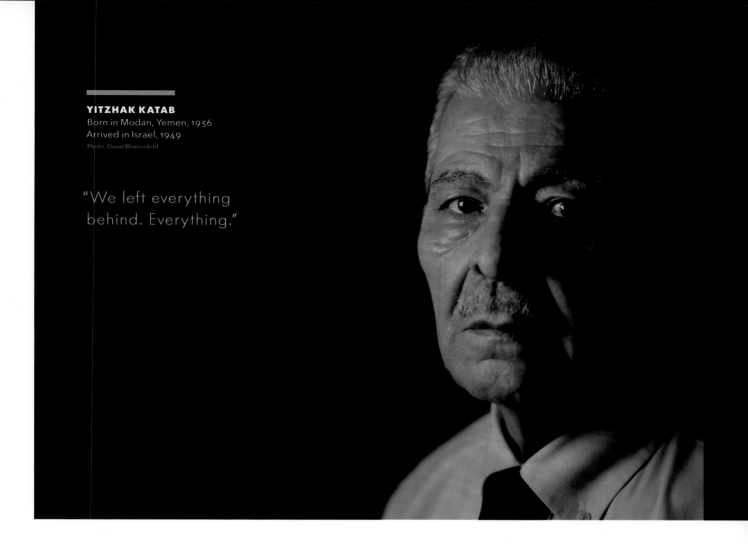

YITZHAK KATAB
Born in Modan, Yemen, 1936
Arrived in Israel, 1949
Photo: David Blumenfeld

"We left everything
behind. Everything."

It was a small village, about twenty-five families, and we all lived in houses made of clay. There were about 180 people and four synagogues. A synagogue for the Katab family, a synagogue for the Libi family, a synagogue for the Oved family, and a synagogue for the Gahali family. Four families lived in peace, lived like brothers all those years. We were not rich, or poor, living a relatively good life.

We came to Israel because we yearned for it from our faith. We left everything behind. Everything. Whatever will be will be. We will get to Israel.

By the end of Operation Magic Carpet, 50,000 Jews had fled Yemen. Only about 3,000 remained. The ancient community had become nearly invisible.

STEVE ACRE (SABIH AZRA EREB)
Born in Baghdad, Iraq, 1932
Arrived in Canada, 1956
Photo: Liam Sharp

"What the hell did
I do as a nine-year-
old that they want
to kill me?"

OPERATION EZRA AND NEHEMIAH

In Iraq, a similar exodus took place. The situation there had been deteriorating for some time, beginning with the terrible events of the Farhud in 1941. Steve Acre, who was then a boy of nine, recalled the wave of killing and looting. "I climbed the tree. It was about fifteen feet high and I was hiding... to see what was happening outside. I saw a lot of men with swords in their hands and with rifles... they're shouting 'Kill the Jews, kill the Jews.' And I was saying to myself, 'What the hell did I do as a nine-year-old that they want to come kill me?'"

Fortunately, the mob was prevented from entering Acre's house by their Muslim landlord. Instead, they went to the neighbor's house, where Acre could hear "screams of the women being raped [and] mutilated." After that day, he said, "I realized that this is no place for me."

When the State of Israel was created, violence against the Jews began again and Acre, now sixteen, decided to escape. Disguised as a Muslim, he made his way from Baghdad to Basra, where he tried and failed twice to cross the border to Iran. On the third effort, "there was an Arab... who took all sixteen of us in

◄ Yemeni immigrants at Giv'at Ye'arim, Israel, proudly display their identity cards while waiting at polling booths, 1951.
Photo: David Eldan / Government Press Office (Israel)

◄ At the height of Operation Ezra and Nehemiah in 1951, planes carrying immigrants from Iraq and Kurdistan landed at Lod Airport (Ben Gurion Airport) about every three hours.
Photo: Teddy Brauner / Government Press Office (Israel)

▲ Shlomo Hillel posed as Richard Armstrong, an American pilot with the Near East Transport Company, to fly Jews out of Iraq.
Courtesy of Shlomo Hillel

a small truck. He was driving to the border, but from far he saw the police, the border police, so he stopped. He says 'Get out of here ... I'll come pick you up in a couple of hours.'" The Arab never came back.

They began to walk east toward Iran. Eventually, they found "some *falahim*, some farmers, and the other men made a deal with them ... to take us across the river. For two nights we had to stay on the farms. They brought us food, bread, and rice. On the third night, they put us in a *balam*, a little boat. We lay down and they put hay on us."

On the other side of the river, they were greeted by Jews who moved them on to the Jewish Cemetery in Teheran and from there by air to Israel. The departure of Acre and his companions from Iran was part of Operation Ezra and Nehemiah, which ultimately airlifted 120,000 Jews out of Iraq. The operation was named after the prophets who had led the Jewish people out of captivity in Babylon in the fifth century BCE.

Operation Ezra and Nehemiah was the culmination of Shlomo Hillel's (facing) work smuggling Jews out of Iraq. Born in Baghdad in 1923, he joined his brothers in Israel when he was eleven, finished school there, joined a kibbutz, and became involved in manufacturing weapons for Haganah, the underground Israeli army that ultimately became the core of the Israel Defense Forces.

In 1946, Hillel joined the Mossad LeAliyah Bet, an arm of Haganah that specialized in smuggling Jews. It began by bringing Jews illegally into Palestine during the British mandate. After the establishment of the State of Israel, it continued its work smuggling Jews out of increasingly draconian and dangerous Arab countries.

SHLOMO HILLEL
Born in Baghdad, Iraq, 1923
Arrived in Israel, 1933
Photo: David Blumenfeld

"We had only one request: when people arrive from Iraq, they will not be returned . . . to Iraq because it's [the] gallows [for them]."

Hillel was sent to Iraq in July of 1946 and again in August of 1947. He found the work extremely challenging. He used Arab drivers to smuggle Jews from Baghdad, through the countryside to Jordan and on to Israel. After more than a year, he had managed to get only thirty-eight people out. In the process, two died, five were wounded, and dozens were imprisoned.

The overland route was too difficult and treacherous. His next effort involved the use of two American pilots and their plane to bring out fifty at a time. The plan was for him to move the emigrants to a destination twenty-five kilometers outside of Baghdad, have them board the plane, take off after midnight, and arrive in Israel very early in the morning while the British officers were asleep. For their trouble, the Americans were to be paid $100 per person.

Hillel notes that this time, he only used Jews in the operation. "We would always smuggle via different Arab smugglers or drivers of commercial vehicles or police officers . . . This time I decided that it was too dangerous. It was the first

▲ Shlomo Hillel as a young boy, 1934
Courtesy of Shlomo Hillel

▲▲ The first load of Iraqi
Jewish refugees arrives in
Israel via a C-46 transport
plane, 1947.
Courtesy of Shlomo Hillel

▲ Father Glasberg (*right*),
Shlomo Hillel's partner
in Operation Ezra and
Nehemiah, embraces
Hillel in 1986.
Courtesy of Shlomo Hillel

time we were doing illegal *aliyah* through the air . . . it must be only
our people from the underground pioneer movement."

He managed to make three trips this way, but then the airplane
was commandeered by Haganah to ship heavy weapons into Israel
in preparation for the war that would inevitably come when Palestine was partitioned.

With the outbreak of war and the invasion of Israel by the Arab
armies, the situation of the Jews in Iraq deteriorated further. The
murder of Shafiq Ades was simply the most outrageous attack on
the ancient community. Jews were removed from public life: bankers could no longer offer their services, Jewish government officials
were dismissed from their posts, wealthy Jews were forced to pay
for the Iraqi army, and Zionist affiliation was made a criminal offense.

As the situation became increasingly dire, Hillel was asked to find a way to get
Jews out of Iraq while there was a temporary truce during the war. It seemed an
impossible undertaking. The Arab armies were everywhere; Arab air forces made
flights impossibly dangerous.

Hillel's new method would prove remarkably ingenious and remarkably effective. He teamed up with a well-connected French Catholic priest, Father Glasberg,
and created a plan to smuggle Jews out of Iraq, through the Assyrian Christian
community on the border of Iran. To do so required a deal with the Iranian

police: they had to agree that when the Jews came into Iran they would not be sent back to Iraq. As Hillel notes, "We had only one request: when people arrive from Iraq, they will not be returned ... to Iraq because it's [the] gallows [for them]." The police agreed.

He also needed visas to be able to fly people out of Iraq to a third country. Father Glasberg asked how many visas he would need; Hillel said 250. Glasberg said fine, "give me the names." Hillel did not know the names so he made them up. A week later the French embassy in Tehran had all the visas.

The Jews that were smuggled through the Assyrian Christian community were lodged in the old Jewish cemetery. From there, they flew to Paris and Marseilles and then travelled by boat to Israel. By the end of 1949, 12,000 people had been smuggled out of Iraq.

The treatment of the Jews by the Iraqi government had become a scandal at the United Nations. The criticisms of Iraq were so intense that there was pressure to refuse it loans that were desperately needed to keep the government solvent. The new prime minister, Tawfiq al-Suwaidi, who had been Iraq's ambassador to the UN, was very conscious of the state of international opinion.

One of his first actions upon taking office was to meet with the head of the Jewish community, Yehezkel Shem-Tov, who had gone to school with him and lived next door. Hillel came to the meeting, although nobody knew that he was the organizer of the illegal smuggling operation. It was agreed that the Jews would be allowed to leave. The prime minister thought 7,000 to 8,000 might go. In the end more than 100,000 left, effectively the vast majority of the ancient Babylonian Jewish community. They left on Hillel's airlift, Operation Ezra and Nehemiah.

▲◄ Jews queue at the Meir Taweig Synagogue in Baghdad to waive their Iraqi citizenship, a condition of emigration to Israel, March 1950.
The Oster Visual Documentation Center, ANU–Museum of the Jewish People, courtesy of David Petel, Tel Aviv

▲ Law 12/1951, published in *Al-Waqā'i' Al-'Irāqiyah*, the official Iraq government newspaper for publishing legislation. It is an expansion of the law that froze the assets of Iraqi Jews and stripped them of their citizenship.
Iraqi Jewish Archive / U.S. National Archives and Records Administration

TRANSLATION: "Law No. 12 for year 1951 Appendix law to the Law for Supervision and Administration of the assets of Jews who were stripped of the Iraqi nationality No. 5 for year 1951

"First Article: From the date of applying this law, the assets of Iraqi Jews who left Iraq with passports, from the first day of 1948, will be frozen and the provisions of law 5 and all the regulations issued or will be issued according to it will apply to them."
Translation by David Khedher Bass-on

By the end of 1952 only about 6,000 Jews were left in Iraq. The Babylonian Jews had disappeared almost completely from their 3,000-year-old home.

A SIMILAR MIGRATION took place out of Syria, following a pogrom in Damascus in 1949, with almost 30,000 Jews crossing the border to Lebanon and on to Israel.

Joseph Abouti's father, who had been arrested as a spy, was one of them: "He was in jail for three months. They took him to Damascus. Finally his friend was able to release him and help him escape immediately to Lebanon." At the time, Abouti was living on a kibbutz. "Shimon Peres [the future prime minister and president of Israel] was a member of the kibbutz. I mentioned to him that my parents had escaped from Syria and were in Lebanon, and could he do anything for them. Sure enough, he exchanged them with prisoners of war, Lebanese soldiers." Abouti's parents arrived in Israel with nothing.

In Libya, at the same time, more than 30,000 Jews left, and in Egypt, 25,000. Even in Iran, where the Persian Jews were relatively well treated, 25,000 left in 1950 and 1951. In total, almost 400,000 Jews left their homes in Arab countries and Iran during the first great exodus after the Israeli War of Independence. Roughly 300,000 went to Israel and the rest to Canada, France, the U.K., Italy, and the United States. These great waves of emigration largely depopulated the most ancient Jewish communities, although more displacement and dispossession was yet to come.

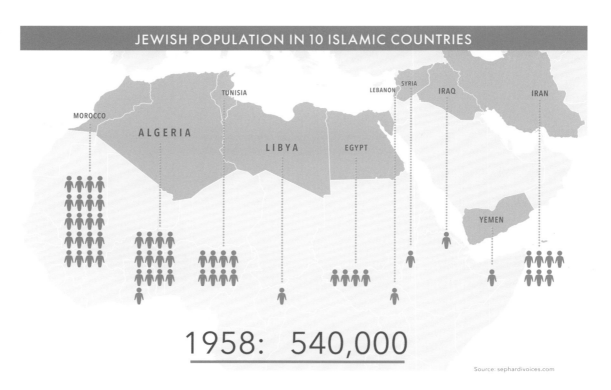

JEWISH POPULATION IN 10 ISLAMIC COUNTRIES

1958: 540,000

Source: sephardivoices.com

JULIETTE AKOUKA GLASSER
Born in Cairo, Egypt, 1941
Arrived in United States, 1959
Photo: Tomas Lopez

"I still have nightmares
[from] the revolution
in 1952."

DECOLONIZATION AND ARAB NATIONALISM

By 1956, almost half the Jews in Arab lands had fled to Israel, France, and North America. Unlike the Palestinians displaced in the War of Independence, they had no status. No provision was made to assist them financially or in any other way. They were left to fend for themselves.

The departure of the 25,000 Jews from Egypt still left a substantial Jewish population. The pressure on those who remained continued, driven on by the Muslim Brotherhood's violent anti-Semitism.

On January 26, 1952, inspired by Hassan al-Banna, the Muslim Brotherhood's founder, thousands of Egyptians rampaged through Cairo attacking Jews and their property. In what came to be called Black Saturday, they destroyed today's equivalent of almost $1 billion (U.S.) worth of Jewish houses and businesses.

Juliette Akouka Glasser (above) recalls the terror of that day. "I still have nightmares [from] during the revolution in 1952. I was very young, very little, and the city was black. There were fires everywhere. And I remember the Arab, the Muslim, the Egyptian walking in the streets, holding big knives, saying, 'We're going

◄ Gamal Abdel Nasser, president of Egypt, speaks to crowds, c. 1956. Nasser led the 1952 overthrow of the monarchy and introduced far-reaching land reforms the following year.

World History Archive / Alamy Stock Photo

◄ Dr. Moussa Marzouk, a house surgeon of French nationality, and Samuel Azar, a teacher, were among the members of a Zionist spy ring sentenced to death by a military court and hanged in Cairo on January 31, 1955.

Keystone Press / Alamy Stock Photo

to kill the Jews. Where are the Jews? Any Jews around here?' And we would hide in the basement. Turn all the lights off. Just shivering, shaking from fear, of fear."

Six months later, the government changed dramatically when the Free Officers Movement, led by General Muhammad Neguib and Colonel Gamal Abdel Nasser, ousted King Farouk and forced him into exile. The new administration attempted to set a more tolerant tone. General Neguib visited Jewish schools and synagogues. Some property that had been confiscated during the War of Independence was returned to Jews still in Egypt.

In June 1954, Nasser became president. A month after he came to power, the relationship to Israel and the Jewish population became poisoned as a result of the badly conceived Levon Affair.

Mossad, the Israeli secret service, hatched a scheme designed to implicate the Muslim Brotherhood in acts of terrorism. They planted bombs at British, French, and Egyptian targets and attempted to make them look like a Muslim Brotherhood operation. The bombs exploded, although nobody was injured or killed. Nine Israeli agents, all of whom were Egyptian Jews, were arrested. One was killed in prison, another committed suicide; the rest were tried, and two were hanged. Nasser's more tolerant policy toward the Jews of Egypt came to an end. The government began another series of arrests of Jewish men.

THE SUEZ CRISIS

Two years later, another blow was struck to Jewish life in Egypt. The Suez Canal and land on both sides of it had been under British control since the end of World War II. It was a fundamental goal of the new government, as a matter of nationalist pride, to gain control over the canal. On July 20, 1956, Nasser announced that it was being nationalized.

Once again, the Israeli government hatched a secret plan, this time with France and Britain, that would further erode the situation of the Egyptian Jews. They all agreed that Israel should move troops toward the Suez Canal, ostensibly in response to terror attacks. France and Britain would then call on Israel to halt its advance and land their own troops at Port Said to "protect" the canal. It was, of course, just an attempt by the old imperial powers to regain control.

Not surprisingly, the resulting Suez Crisis, also known as the Second Arab-Israeli War, fanned the flames of anti-Israel and anti-Jewish feeling in Egypt. Hundreds of Jews were arrested and the government passed a law, the Egyptian Nationality Code, that barred all so-called Zionists from Egyptian nationality. It went on to make clear that all Jews were Zionists and, therefore, enemies of the state.

David Shama (page 72) was born in Cairo, Egypt, in 1945. He describes how far the situation of the Jews had deteriorated: "My father was a businessman.

Scuttled ships at the entrance
to the Suez Canal, at Port Said,
November 19, 1956
AP Photo

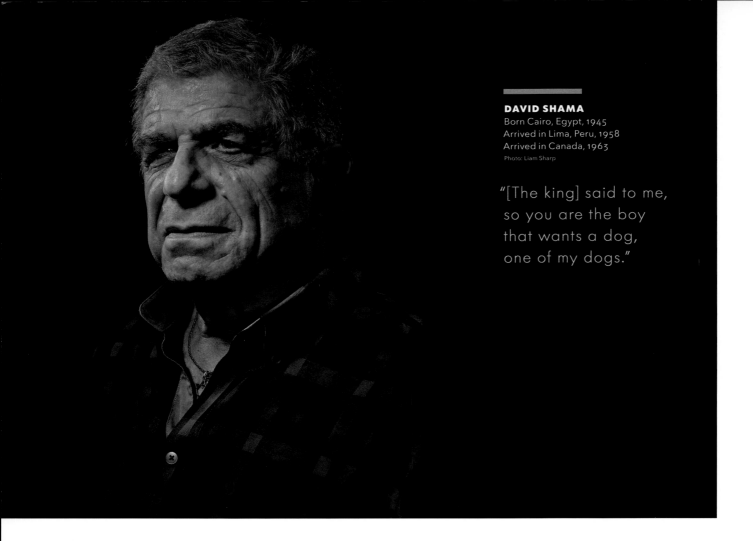

DAVID SHAMA
Born Cairo, Egypt, 1945
Arrived in Lima, Peru, 1958
Arrived in Canada, 1963
Photo: Liam Sharp

"[The king] said to me,
so you are the boy
that wants a dog,
one of my dogs."

David Shama's parents,
Eva Salama and Isaac Shama,
at their wedding in
Alexandria, 1931
Courtesy of David Shama

[We were] an affluent family with many servants, chauffeurs, gardeners, a life of opulence in every way. My parents were fully integrated; we believed they were fully accepted. I can't remember my mother ever saying she suffered from racism."

So well connected was the family, he says, that "on my ninth birthday my father came into my room and asked, 'What would you like for your birthday?' I immediately replied a dog. My father said we're getting you the perfect dog. We're going to King Farouk's Montaza Palace... I had never been to the palace... [When we arrived,] my father said it's the king... I bowed and my father bowed too... [The king] said to me, so you are the boy that wants a dog, one of my dogs. I said yes your majesty. He then summoned an officer to take me to the kennels to pick a puppy. The officer told me to pick a puppy. And so I did."

The Shamas' life of opulence and connections to the highest parts of society came undone after the outbreak of the Suez Crisis. "My father received a call to come down to the precinct. Our chauffeur drove him there and waited in front of the station, but my father never came out; he just disappeared off the face of the earth. It took several weeks to find out he was accused of being a spy for the

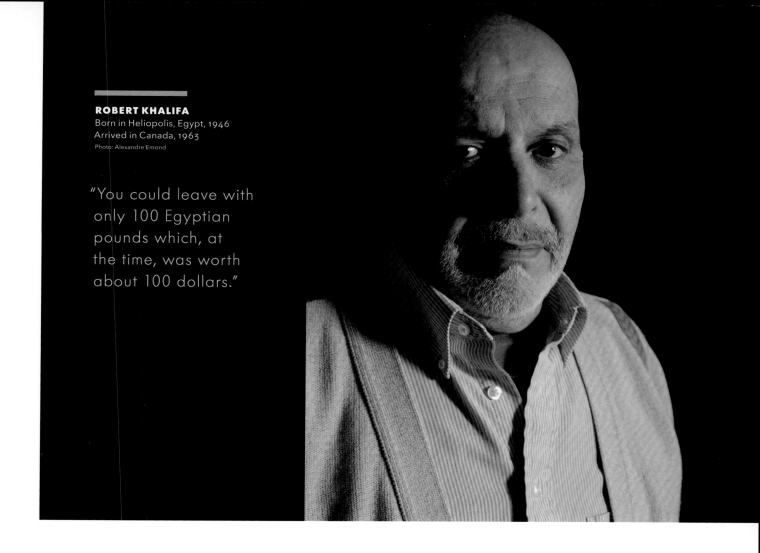

"You could leave with only 100 Egyptian pounds which, at the time, was worth about 100 dollars."

British government and Israel... My mother used to go out every night alone... from jail to jail searching for him... Our bank accounts were frozen, so she took her jewelry [to bribe the guards]."

David's father was tortured. On the day of his trial, he pled innocence and was taken to an adjoining room and beaten until he told them he would plead guilty. "I was in the courtroom that day sitting beside my mother, holding her hand. I remember the judge asking my father, who could hardly stand, are you guilty or innocent, and my father replied guilty." He was sentenced "to be killed by a firing squad."

David and his mother returned home and were assaulted by the police in their house. A few days later, men came to the front door. There was "an individual covered from head to toe... They removed the blanket. It was my father... The guy who brought him to the house said you have twenty-four hours at the most to get out of the country because they will find he's missing."

Their loyal chauffeur made an arrangement with a fisherman that very night to help them escape by boat. They spent two days at sea covered in fishing nets

ANDRÉ ACIMAN
Born in Alexandria, Egypt, 1951
Arrived in Rome, 1965
Arrived in the United States, 1968
Photo: Rosdiana Ciaravolo / Getty Images

"But you are a dog of the Arabs."

and tarpaulins, unable to move. After being picked up by a freighter, the Shamas arrived in Marseilles. They arrived with nothing but the clothes they were wearing. David's father was a broken man.

David Shama's family was joined by thousands more fleeing Egypt after the Suez Crisis. They left any way they could: by air, by sea, or by land. They left with nothing—their property was confiscated and their assets frozen.

Robert Khalifa (page 73) explains that "when you left and you had a company, you had a business, that automatically became the property of Egypt. You could leave with only 100 Egyptian pounds which, at the time, was worth about 100 dollars."

For those who stayed on, the situation did not improve. If anything, it became worse. Jews still had to wear distinctive clothing and were subject to arbitrary arrest. In 1961, the government seized almost 800 Jewish businesses.

André Aciman (above), the distinguished literary critic and novelist (*Call Me By Your Name*), left in 1964 at age thirteen. He was at that time the last Jewish student in his school. His teacher assigned him a poem to memorize that vilified

Jews. When a classmate called him "Kalb al-Arab"—a dog of the Arabs—he complained to his teacher. As he later recalled, "She did not give me time to finish my complaint. 'But you are a dog of the Arabs,' she replied in Arabic, smiling as though it were the most obvious thing in the world."[8]

By 1968, almost all the Jews had left Egypt. Where there had been more than 75,000 at the end of World War II, there were only 2,500 left. The communities that dated back to Moses and the Great Library at Alexandria during the Hellenistic era were gone—their synagogues were abandoned, their houses and businesses forfeited, and their ancient culture scattered to the wind.

RIPPLES FROM THE SUEZ

The Suez Crisis aggravated the Arab countries' sense of betrayal by the colonial powers and their distaste for Israel and their own Jewish populations. As they gained independence, the ability of France and Britain to limit the harsher impulses of the new governments vanished. In most cases, independence brought with it severe crackdowns on local Jews.

When Tunisia became independent in 1956, its new ruler, Habib Bourghiba, had no particular animosity toward Jews and even had one in his first cabinet. Despite Bourghiba's tolerant attitude, however, the new government, pressured by rising Muslim extremism, moved against its own Jews. In 1958, it announced a policy of "Arabization" that ensured priority in jobs and services to Muslims.

The exclusion of the Jews in public and commercial life was followed by arrests. Within a few years of Tunisian independence, 70,000 Jews had fled their

Jews of the Atlas Mountains, Morocco, 1949
Courtesy of the Central Zionist Archives

homes. More than half went to Israel and 30,000 went to Tunisia's old colonial master, France.

In Morocco, before independence and under French rule, official policy was to allow Jews to live relatively unmolested. Nevertheless, a number of Jewish agencies set up arrangements to facilitate their departure. In 1954 and 1955, more than 33,000 Jews left, tired of attacks by Muslims.

When Morocco became independent in 1956, the new government of Sultan Sidi ben Youssef moved, as one of its first acts, to block the emigration of Jewish Moroccans. The government described Jewish emigration as "a betrayal and desertion of Morocco... It is unjust that Moroccans should take the place of Palestinian Arabs in Israel. And that is why we stop the Jews leaving."[9]

To counter the Moroccan government, Mossad created an underground organization to get the Jews out of the country. It shepherded them secretly hundreds of kilometers across the desert to Spanish Morocco. From there they traveled under cover of darkness to Marseilles and—for many—on to Israel. Between 1956 and 1961, more than 35,000 Jews left Morocco clandestinely.

The government was not pleased. Nevertheless, secret negotiations began between King Mohammed V's son and successor, King Hassan II, and the Israeli government. The deal that was eventually reached required Israel to pay Morocco $100 for each emigrant. Over the next three years, Israel paid $10 million to bring a further 100,000 Jews to safety.

Between 1948 and 1968, a mere twenty years, the largest Jewish population in any Arab country left. Where there had been 265,000 Jews in Morocco, the successive waves of emigration had reduced it by 215,000 people. Like Egypt and Tunisia, the ancient Jewish communities of Morocco simply vanished, the people themselves landing principally in Canada, France, and Israel.

PRESSURE IN THE MIDDLE EAST

The restrictions on Jews leaving was not unique to the newly independent countries of North Africa. Syria, which had been independent since the end of World War II, refused to let its Jews emigrate. The government's reasoning was similar to Morocco's: they did not want Syrian Jews going to Israel to strengthen its population.

There were occasional brief liftings of the ban on emigration, but Jews could only leave if they agreed to abandon all their assets and depart penniless. These windows were short and by 1959 they had closed altogether. The Syrian Jews were effectively captives, imprisoned in their own country.

The situation in Iraq was no better. In 1963, the Ba'ath Party came to power and with it came further restrictions on the lives of the remaining Jews. Like their Syrian counterparts, they were not allowed to travel abroad, they were excluded from the universities, and their property was confiscated. The 1,000-year-old Jewish cemetery in Baghdad was also destroyed.

Naim Dangoor came from a distinguished Jewish family. His grandfather had been the chief rabbi of Iraq. They traced their heritage back hundreds of years. He had been exceptionally successful in the 1940s and '50s. With his Muslim partner and friend, Ahmed Safwat, he had founded Eastern Industries in Baghdad. Their businesses encompassed everything from match and furniture factories to real estate and the Coca-Cola concession for Iraq.

His house was on the Tigris River across from the royal palace. He was so well connected socially that he was invited to New Year's Eve parties with the royal family. At one of these events, the guests were in the process of selecting Miss Baghdad. They had reduced the number of candidates to five finalists. When the Dangoors arrived, the regent insisted that the final five must include a sixth, Renée, Naim's wife-to-be (they were courting and married eleven months later). That evening she was crowned Miss Baghdad.

Despite his wealth and brilliant connections, Naim Dangoor was very concerned about the future for the Jews in Iraq. In 1960, he moved his family to the United Kingdom. He, however, continued to run his businesses in Iraq. For the next three years, he shuttled between London and Baghdad, attempting to keep his business going. When he did not return to Iraq in 1963 to renew his passport, a special law for Jews meant that he lost his

▲ The Dangoor family, 1939, including Naim Dangoor (*standing, right*) and Abdullah Dangoor (*seated, right*)
Courtesy of David Dangoor

citizenship, along with all his assets. In effect, the Iraqi government stole his house, his bank accounts, and his businesses.

Like so many others, after 2,500 years, there was no longer any place for the Babylonian Jews in Babylon.

In November of 1963, the Ba'ath Party fell from power. The restrictions on Jews were lifted and they began once more to look forward, hoping the worst was over. But the brief interregnum would not last. After the Six-Day War, the Ba'ath Party would return, bringing with it the horrors of more repression and the murderous Saddam Hussein.

THE ALGERIAN REVOLUTION

The tide of Arab nationalism that engulfed the rest of North Africa engulfed Algeria as well. It was, however, a special case. The most populous part, the Mediterranean coastal region, was part of France and voted twenty-seven representatives from its three departments to the National Assembly in Paris.

The problem was that not all the inhabitants of Algeria were equal. The Jews, since the Crémieux Decree of 1870, were citizens, as were the settlers from France (known as the *colons*, and later called the Pieds-Noirs). Together they constituted just over a million of the five million people living in French Algeria in 1955.

CHARLES DIAINE
Born in Algiers, Algeria, 1939
Arrived in France, 1961
Photo: Vincent Devries

"For sure [Algeria]
was our country,
for generations and
generations."

The Arab Muslims were another matter. When the Jews had been made into French citizens in 1870, they had not. They could apply individually, but had to renounce Islam. Even when they did, very few were granted citizenship.

Inevitably these arrangements led to bitterness. The privileged Pieds-Noirs dominated the French government's view of how to deal with Algeria for decades, largely ignoring the needs of their Arab neighbors. As time went on, the Jews increasingly identified with the Pieds-Noirs, becoming more and more French in outlook and attachment.

The case of Charles Diaine's (above) father reflected this tendency. Émile Diaine was born into grinding poverty in Algiers during World War I. He grew up in the Casbah, where his neighbors were overwhelmingly Arabs and Jews. He lived with his family in a tiny apartment without toilets, running water, or electricity. Rats scurried up and down the staircase.

Émile Diaine (*kneeling, centre left*) worked as a carpenter at city hall in Algiers in the 1940s.
Courtesy of Charles Diaine

GISLAINE LEVY DIAINE
Born in Philippeville, Algeria, 1946
Arrived in Lyon, France, 1961
Photo: Vincent Devries

"I always lived with
this fear of being
assaulted."

Gislaine Levy (*standing, right*),
1954   Courtesy of Gislaine Diaine

He felt so strongly that he belonged to France that he joined a French regiment in 1939 to fight the Germans. He and his fellow soldiers were captured almost immediately and interned in a prisoner-of-war camp in Europe. He had never told anyone that he was Jewish. When German officers came through the camp, they saw him without clothes and noted that he was circumcised. The French officer swore to the Germans, on his honor as an officer, that he was not Jewish. They accepted his word.

After the end of the war, the frustration of the Arabs reached a boiling point. Their underground army, the Front de Libération Nationale (FLN) initiated the Algerian struggle for independence by attacking French troops in November of 1954. The French military responded with extraordinary savagery, in the end defeating the FLN at the Battle of Algiers in 1958. The Arab civilian population paid a terrible price.

Gislaine Levy Diaine (above), the wife of Charles Diaine, grew up in Algeria at this time. "Because my name is Levy, it is a billboard that I am Jewish. When I was little in Algeria, [my] girlfriends were anti-Semitic. I always lived with this fear of being assaulted. Being attacked by Muslims."

The FLN carried on the struggle using guerilla tactics. Widespread atrocities were committed by both sides. The war became so cruel that the French public turned against it, resulting in the collapse of the Fourth Republic and the emergence of Charles de Gaulle as the new president of France.

The Pieds-Noirs were determined to keep Algeria as an integral part of France. De Gaulle went to Algiers in June of 1958 to address them and the rest of the country on the future of Algeria. Famously, he said that he understood them: "Je vous ai compris." They took it that he meant that he agreed with them; he meant the opposite.

When his "betrayal" became clear, the Pieds-Noirs organized their own underground army, the Organisation de l'Armée Secrète (OAS), which pursued a campaign of terror in both Algeria and mainland France.

Charles Diaine managed to escape the terrible poverty of his parents and won a scholarship to the École Normale Supérieure in Paris. As he notes in his Sephardi Voices interview, the school's most famous student, Albert Camus, a Pied-Noir and winner of the Nobel Prize in Literature, had studied in the same library as he did.

When the Algerian Revolution broke out, he took a year to get his teaching certificate and began working at an Arab school in the Casbah. Because he was seen as Pied-Noir, his life was constantly threatened. The principal of the school, an Arab, told him he had to leave or he would be killed. The only way out of Algeria was to join the French army. He did, but found himself in an increasingly difficult situation. He was the sole Algerian Jew, the only Pied-Noir in his regiment.

▲ French President Charles de Gaulle greets crowds in Saïda during a visit to Algeria on August 28, 1959.
AP Photo / God

▼◄ Charles Diaine (*middle row, third from the left*) as a boy in the École Publique de la Rue du Divan in Algiers, 1946
Courtesy of Charles Diaine

▼ Charles Diaine as a teacher in Algiers, November 23, 1960
Courtesy of Charles Diaine

He believed in Algerian independence, which put him at odds with his fellow soldiers (many of whom were anti-Semites) and the OAS. At the same time, the FLN despised all the members of the French army, particularly the Pied-Noir members.

Ultimately his regiment found itself 500 kilometers from Algiers and his family when independence was declared in 1962. The declaration created a panic among the Pieds-Noirs and the Jews. They feared that as the Arabs took control of the country, there would be reprisals. They were not wrong. Thousands fled to the harbor to try to escape to France. The OAS threw bombs into the crowd to try to force them to stay. Fear and terror reigned.

Charles Diaine's parents managed to get out, but had to leave everything behind, except his two siblings and two suitcases. All of Diaine's books, diplomas, and photos were abandoned in their apartment in the Casbah.

Over 900,000 Pieds-Noirs left Algeria, of whom 125,000 were Jews. Some 100,000 of the Jews went to France and the rest went to Israel. The departure of the Jews from Algeria left many feeling bitter, not just because of their dispossession, but even more centrally of their homeland.

As Charles Diaine explains, "For sure [Algeria] was our country for generations and generations... We don't even know how long we have been there. It's only by chance that we became French. If the French had not come in 1830, we would have remained Jews of Algeria. It was chance that made us French... and what it produced was war and so many crimes and deaths that reconciliation was impossible between the Algerians and the Arabs."

THE EXODUS CONTINUES: 1967–1980

"They were killing Jewish people, Jewish families."

MARIA MEGHNAGI ARON

The following signs appear in the photograph:

12 AIN AOUDA

HAD-el-BRACHOUA-20
ROMMANI 43

4 **THE TENSIONS ASSOCIATED** with the results of the Israeli War of Independence never dissipated. The defeated Arab countries—Iraq, Syria, Jordan and Egypt—refused to accept the existence of a Jewish state in Palestine. The Israelis felt vulnerable within the narrow geography of their small state; they feared it would be almost impossible to defend in any future attack.

These tensions came to a head in May of 1967 when President Nasser of Egypt imposed a naval blockade on the Straits of Tiran, cutting off Israel's access to the Red Sea. This was seen as a provocation that could not be ignored, since it was, in effect, an act of war. The mood in the Middle East became very dark; another war was seen as inevitable.

In the Arab capitals and among Palestinian Arabs, there was general enthusiasm for war and confidence that Israel would lose badly. The Arab leaders were not wrong to be confident. Their combined forces were far superior, numerically, to that of the Israelis, with four times as many combat planes, five times as many tanks, and nearly twice as many men.

Jimmy Benaudis at age fifteen (*left, sitting*) with four French-Canadian friends, somewhere between Aïn El Aouda and Rommani, Morocco, 1975
Courtesy of Jimmy Benaudis

THE SIX-DAY WAR

On June 5, 1967, Israel preemptively attacked the Egyptian air force. It caught the vast majority of its planes on the ground, destroying 286 of them and killing a third of Egypt's pilots. For the rest of the war, Israel would enjoy overwhelming air superiority. On the second and third days of the war, one of the great tank battles of history took place between Egypt and Israel. The Egyptian army in Sinai was crushed, in large part because of Israel's dominance of the skies.

Jordan entered the war in support of the Egyptians, but with too little, too late. The Israeli army drove the Jordanians out of Jerusalem and out of the West Bank, all the way to the Jordan River. In the course of the war, the Israelis seized the Golan Heights, dramatically reducing Syria's ability to attack Israel.

Jimmy Benaudis (facing) was born in Tangier in 1960. He recalls how, even though he was only seven years old, the Six-Day War became a turning point for him:

It was probably the first time in my life that I felt my Jewish identity and anti-Semitism. It was in June 1967. I was at school; it was second grade. All the students in my class were my friends and they were everything… mostly French and Muslim, the majority were Muslim.

All of a sudden, the Six-Day War breaks out. It's the middle of the school day. [At recess] a few kids from my class, seven years old, came at noon, came at me, saying, "We are going to kill you because you are a Jew, you're a Zionist."

JIMMY BENAUDIS
Born in Tangier, Morocco, 1960
Arrived in France, 1978
Arrived in the United States, 2012
Photo: Tomas Lopez

"We are going to kill
you because you're a
Jew . . . a Zionist."

◄ Jimmy Benaudis (*top
row, third from right*) with
his second-grade class
at École André Chénier,
which included four Jewish
children, thirteen Muslims,
and sixteen Christians, 1967
Courtesy of Jimmy Benaudis

MARIA MEGHNAGI ARON
Born in Tripoli, Libya, 1945
Arrived in Rome, 1967
Arrived in Israel, 1971
Photo: David Blumenfeld

"Everything was
confiscated: the
houses, the business,
the bank account.
We had nothing.
Nothing."

Maria Aron was born in Tripoli, Libya, in 1945. She recalls the impact of the war on her family. On Friday, June 3, two days before the war began, they fled for safety to Italy:

Friday morning, my mother started to prepare for Shabbat. My brother said, "Pack your luggage." So I took one bag. So did my parents. We flew to Rome. On June 6, we were in Rome and heard on the radio that the war between Israel and the Arab countries had started. We heard that they were burning all the Jewish stores and going into the houses in Tripoli. They were killing Jewish people, Jewish families. We heard that Tripoli was on fire. For a week, we didn't know whether my brother was dead or alive. Everything was confiscated: the houses, the business, the bank account. We had nothing. Nothing.

Six days after the war began, the Israelis were victorious on all fronts. They had an unprecedented and stunning outcome. Israel now controlled land covering an area four and a half times greater than its prewar size. The Egyptian army—the largest and most important of the Arab armies—had lost 85 percent of its military hardware. The Arabs had been thoroughly and completely humiliated.

During the war, more Palestinian Arabs were displaced. Somewhere between 200,000 to 300,000 people fled their homes as the Israelis advanced into the West Bank. Many of them had been driven out of their lands and villages before, during the War of Independence.

Three months after the war ended, the World Islamic Congress met in Amman, the capital of Jordan. In a statement about the Jews living in Arab countries the organization chose words that were full of threat: "The Congress is certain that the Jewish communities living in Islamic countries do not appreciate the Muslims' good treatment and protection over the centuries. The Congress declares that the Jews residing in Arab countries who contact the Zionist circles or the State of Israel do not deserve the protection and care which Islam provides." These Jews were warned that "Islamic governments should treat them as aggressive combatants. Similarly, the Islamic peoples, individually and collectively, should boycott them and treat them as deadly enemies."[10]

The pressure intensified against the remaining Jews in North Africa and the Middle East, leading to the almost total absence of Jews in these countries within a few years.

Israel after the Six-Day War, which ended June 10, 1967
Credit: Eric Leinberger

IRAQ

In Iraq, the Ba'ath Party regained power in July 1968. Repressive measures against the 5,000 remaining Jews were intensified. In October, the government announced that it had uncovered a spy network operating on behalf of Zionism and imperialism. Of the sixteen Jews who were arrested, seven died under torture in prison and the other nine were executed.

The murdered Jews' bodies were hung in Tahrir Square in central Baghdad. The Iraqi government declared the day a national holiday, and an estimated one million people went to see the bodies. As Martin Gilbert describes it, "Crowds of Baghdadis surrounded the gallows, dancing, chanting and even picnicking."[11]

The crackdown on the Jews led to a further exodus. Edwin Shuker (page 91) escaped in 1971 at the age of sixteen. His grandparents had left twenty years earlier in the 1951 exodus organized by Shlomo Hillel. His father had stayed on to finish his law degree, hoping that the worst was past.

As Shuker describes it, however, by 1968 life in Iraq had "become a living hell." The forced "confessions" of the Jewish "spies" had resulted in the naming

Sabah Haim and David
Hazaquiel, both Jewish
businessmen accused
of spying for Israel, were
hanged in Baghdad on
January 27, 1969.
AP Photo

of Christian and Muslim friends, with catastrophic results for their families. Nobody wanted to be associated with the Jews any longer. The gulf between the Jewish and other communities became unbridgeable. Jewish and non-Jewish families stayed apart; children were no longer allowed to go to each other's houses.

Shuker's family spoke Judaeo-Arabic, but restricted it to home, relatives, and close friends. When they went out to shop, or to the park or any public place, they used only the local dialect, for fear that they would be identified as Jews.

The climate of anxiety and repression grew worse and worse. Jews were routinely rounded up, imprisoned, tortured, and executed. It became a criminal offense to listen to the Israeli broadcasts in Arabic. The local newspaper published the names and addresses of Jews who were "doing unusual things." Everyone lived in fear to see if their names were on the list.

Eventually Shuker's father was arrested, as well "as everybody else ... my mother pleaded for his life with someone who was powerful enough and that person told her to leave the house and never come back or even mention his

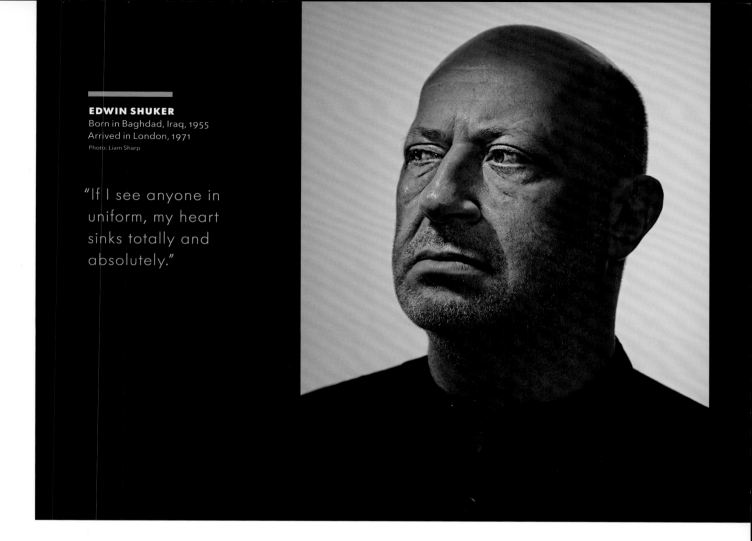

EDWIN SHUKER
Born in Baghdad, Iraq, 1955
Arrived in London, 1971
Photo: Liam Sharp

"If I see anyone in uniform, my heart sinks totally and absolutely."

name." His father was released by the "powerful person," however, who warned the family: "This is the last time you ever see me or hear me."

By this time, everyone was attempting to escape, but "Saddam Hussein's men were on every corner." Shuker estimates that between a quarter and half of all the men in his community were arrested. They were inevitably tortured. "Torture by Saddam Hussein and his henchmen [was] what they did. I don't know any other place that had such sophistication, such cruelty, and such sadism as the Ba'ath Party had from 1968 to 2003."

Finally, in August of 1971, his father gathered the family and said, "We have two hours in this house and we will be gone." Shuker recalls, "We spent the two hours just roaming around . . . I remember going up and down looking at all my collections, one at a time, saying goodbye to them." They left everything behind.

They took the night train to Mosul, in Kurdistan. It was packed. None of the children were allowed to speak. They were traveling on forged papers. They were in constant fear that their papers would be checked, and found to be fraudulent.

Edwin Shuker (*second from right*) at a school party, Baghdad, c. 1970
Courtesy of Edwin Shuker

Shuker feared that they would "be marched out... dragged out by our hair... and be tortured to death." When they arrived at Mosul, they managed to convince a taxi driver to take them north. They traveled through endless checkpoints, each time terrified that their fake papers would be discovered.

The fear was so tremendous that forty years later Shuker can still not shake it off. "I mean till today, till now, if I see anyone in uniform, my heart sinks totally and absolutely. At my age. Today. After forty years being here [London]... if I see a policeman, even though he's not even asking to talk to me, just a police car, my heart just completely and totally sinks. And when he stops me, I'm shaking..."

In the Kurdish territories, they met a man who would smuggle them into Iran. By then, however, "there were twenty people in the car, twenty-two people... we were packed on top of one another. There were no lights. The cars had to drive completely in darkness. The valley was down below. There were no barriers, no nothing." Strangely, the Kurd who smuggled them into Iran was Masoud Barzani, the son of the legendary Mustafa Barzani and a future president of Kurdistan.

Eventually Shuker made it to London, where his uncle lived. He enrolled at university the Sunday following the outbreak of the Yom Kippur War. While he waited in line to register he learned he may have escaped Baghdad, but that didn't necessarily mean he was safe:

I heard the chilling voices behind me of Iraqis speaking in the local dialect. Immediately I become very, very nervous. And they noticed that and one of them said... "This guy, I think he understands what we are talking about..." I was filling the form and [they] caught it by force and it says "Born: Baghdad, Iraq." And he said, "You see? I told you." And then they escorted me to the union, where about 200 Arabs are sitting in a dark room watching war videos from the front. And they switched on a light... I cannot describe the fear as [all these] Arabs turned back to see me. And these guys said, "We want to introduce a brother of us, a brother Arab who just arrived." And they said: "You are a Muslim?" So I said then, "No. My mother was English." I was making it up out of sheer terror. And they said, "What's the difference? Muslim, Christian. We are all brothers today. There is a war and the Jews have to be eliminated... and so don't worry about not being a Muslim. You are an Arab."

For the next three years, Shuker had to pretend to be a Christian Arab who didn't like Jews. He did not speak to any Jews for the entire time, constantly afraid that he would be found out.

The departure of Shuker and his family was paralleled by the departure of thousands more, most being smuggled out through the Kurdish territories and into Iran. In all cases, they had to abandon everything they owned; their assets were then seized by the state.

Lisette Shashoua Ades describes a similar experience:

After the 1967 war, our bank accounts were frozen, our houses ransacked. They would take a husband or a child and you would never see them again. One woman's son was taken on the pretense of wanting to ask him a few questions. "We'll bring him back in two hours." Two months later after not being able to visit him in any prison, she was finally able to see him—hanging in the square. When she approached him, crying, the crowd started throwing stones at her, shouting, "She's the mother of a spy."

My Muslim friends stopped talking to me [at the university]. They began reporting on us, lying, saying one drew a Star of David. They punched us in the stomach, told us to leave the country and never come back. They threatened to kill us. These were our colleagues, our friends.

Like the Shukers, Lisette Shashoua escaped using smugglers to get her to Kurdistan and from there across the border into Iran. The terror of the journey has never left her. Fifty years later, she reflects, "The trauma never leaves you. You're always careful, always scared. It was terrifying, horrifying."

By the early 1970s, the once-thriving Jewish community in Iraq was reduced to almost nobody. Where there had been 135,000 people only twenty years earlier, all the Jewish houses, businesses, synagogues, and schools stood empty. The center of Jewish scholarship and intellectual life for 2,600 years was at an end.

Lisette Shashoua (*crouched, center*) in Tehran, November 1970, after escaping from Iraq
Courtesy of Lisette Shashoua

SYRIA

The loss of the Golan Heights to Israel so embittered the government of Syria that it dramatically tightened the restrictions on its Jewish community. The Jews were forbidden from emigrating, subject to 10:00 p.m. curfews, limited to six years of elementary school, barred from jobs in the public service and banks, denied visits by foreigners unless they were accompanied by government officials, denied access to radios, telephones, or postal contact with anyone outside of Syria, and had their property confiscated at death. The Jews became prisoners in their own country, completely cut off from the rest of the world.

Gabrielle Elia (page 94) was living in Lebanon with her father at the time. It was clear even from the neighboring country how extreme the situation in Syria had become.

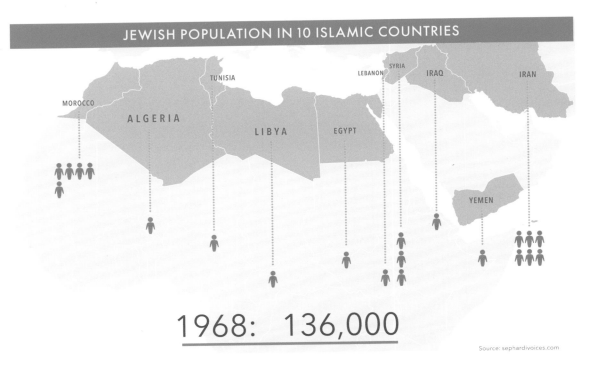

JEWISH POPULATION IN 10 ISLAMIC COUNTRIES

1968: 136,000

Source: sephardivoices.com

THE YOM KIPPUR WAR

On October 6, 1973, Syria and Egypt once again attacked Israel. The joint Syrian-Egyptian code name for the attack was "Badr," named after the Battle of Badr, where Muhammad defeated the Jewish Quarishi tribe at Mecca. They chose Yom Kippur, the Day of Atonement, the holiest day in the Jewish religious calendar, to launch their invasion. The Israeli military and security authorities were taken completely by surprise.

Egyptian forces crossed the Suez Canal and entered the Sinai virtually unopposed. Syria invaded the Golan Heights, which had been captured by Israel during the Six-Day War. The Arab armies made significant advances as the Israelis scrambled to respond. Finally, three days after the beginning of the war, the Israeli army managed to halt their progress, blocking the Egyptian tanks and halting the forward movement of the Syrians.

As day four of the war dawned, the Israelis began to reverse the Arab gains. They drove the Syrians off the Golan and pushed them back beyond the cease-fire lines of the Six-Day War. They penetrated Syria so deeply that they could begin shelling the outskirts of Damascus.

The Egyptian army advance stalled, but managed to take the offensive again, only to find itself in an enormous tank battle in the sands of the Sinai. The Israeli commanders, seeing an opportunity, drove their tanks through an opening between the two major Egyptian tank groups. Penetrating the "seam" allowed the Israelis to bridge the canal and press on to the city of Suez. Before they arrived, the United Nations brokered a cease-fire.

► Syrian Soldiers hold their hands up as a sign of surrender in the Golan Heights, 1973.
Government Press Office (Israel)

▼ A mobile bridge built by the Israel Defense Forces on the Suez Canal, October 25, 1973
Photo: Ron Ilan / Government Press Office (Israel)

On October 22, conflict broke out again, with each side blaming the other. Two days later, the Israelis had encircled the Egyptian Third Army and the city of Suez. They had effectively defeated the Egyptians for a third time. A permanent cease-fire went into effect on October 25.

In Egypt, the end of the war did not result in further reprisals against the Jewish population, since almost all the Egyptian Jews had already left. In Syria, however, the government refused to let the remaining Jews leave, subjecting them to harassment, imprisonment, torture, and execution. Finally, in 1991, President Hafez al-Assad (the father of the current president, Bashir al-Assad) agreed to let the 4,000 Jews who were still there leave—so long as they did not emigrate to Israel.

▲ Egyptian president Anwar Sadat is flanked by chief of staff Sadedin Shazli (*left*) and war minister General Ahmed Ismail as he reviews maps of battle developments in the desert of the Sinai Peninsula, at his army headquarters in Cairo, on October 15, 1973.
AP Photo

Even after all the Jews had gone, persistent, extreme anti-Semitism infected Syria. The defense minister, Mustafa Tlass, published *The Matzah of Zion*, endorsing the ancient blood libel and noting "the religious beliefs of the Jews and the destructive perversions they contain, which draw their orientation from a dark hate towards all humankind and all religions."[12] The Syrian representative to the United Nations Commission on Human Rights recommended the book unreservedly to her colleagues.

Even though Morocco was not a belligerent in the Yom Kippur War, it still affected the Jews there. For Jimmy Benaudis (see page 87), a teenager at the time, the Yom Kippur War deeply reinforced his sense of otherness. He came to believe that there was no place for the Jews any longer in Morocco.

> Morocco got involved in the war. They sent soldiers. We started hearing stories about Moroccan soldiers being even more cruel than the Syrians, like taking Israeli soldiers, cutting off their hands, and putting them in bags to [keep] as souvenirs. It was very, very troubling and very scary.
>
> That was a turning point. We knew that we had possibly no future in Morocco [and] this was it, this was the time we started planning. I can remember very well from '73 to '75, '76, '77 I used to go with my parents to some friends and all the conversations were about "Oh, have you heard that that family left?"

Jimmy Benaudis's high school identity card, Rabat, 1976
Courtesy of Jimmy Benaudis

Nevertheless, Benaudis claims that he enjoyed this time: "I had wonderful teenage years. I have great memories ... I had great friends. But at the same time, we had this feeling that it was not our home, it was not our country. And there was always somebody to make us remember that even in our closest surroundings, even my closest friends, even my best friend would tell me 'You're only a Jew.'"

With regret, he left Morocco. "I graduated high school in 1978. [At the time,] 95 to 99 percent of the Jews graduating high school used to leave." He departed for France the very year he graduated.

Like Morocco, Lebanon was not a belligerent in the Yom Kippur War. Shortly after the end of the war, however, Lebanon fell apart. In 1975, the civil war began, and it would rage for seventeen years, plunging it into an ongoing crisis and destroying the country.

Although there were very few Jews in Lebanon, they were, like their counterparts in the rest of the Middle East, subject to chronic anti-Semitism. Edy Cohen Halala (facing) recalls his childhood growing up in a predominantly Shia neighborhood in Beirut. Despite the fact that Arabic was his first language, he was still, even as a small child, the perpetual maligned outsider.

EDY COHEN HALALA
Born in Beirut, Lebanon, 1972
Arrived in France, 1989
Arrived in Israel, 1995
Photo: David Blumenfeld

"I am a Jew and as
a Jew, I am guilty."

I am a Jew and as a Jew, I am guilty. And what is my fault? I have two
main charges. First, for the Christians, you, you Eddie, killed Jesus. And
Muslims would say to me "You stole Palestine."

Girls did not want to talk to me because I'm Jewish. Their parents
do not allow them to speak or deal with the Jews. As a kid, it's very trou-
bling... you don't know what you've done.

In March of 1985, during the civil war, his father was kidnapped along
with twelve other Lebanese Jews. A group calling itself the Organization of
the Oppressed on Earth claimed responsibility. It sent pictures of four of
its captives, including Edy's father, to the local newspapers and offered to
swap the Jews for hundreds of prisoners held in Israeli jails. The government of Israel refused to negotiate with "terrorists." Edy's father was shot in
the head. He was thirty-nine.

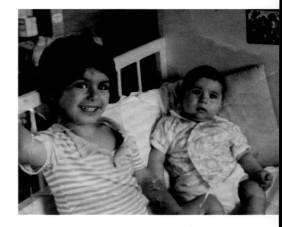

One-year-old Edy Cohen next to
his older brother Robert, 1973
Courtesy of Edy Cohen

LINA ZARGAR SAMIMY
Born in Tehran, Iran, 1938
Arrived in the United States, 1961
Photo: Tomas Lopez

"The Jewish people were always called *najes* . . . somebody who is going to make you dirty if you touch them."

THE IRANIAN REVOLUTION

The regime of the shahs began in 1921 with the ascension of Reza Khan to power, and then to the throne. He was succeeded by his son, Mohammad Reza Pahlavi, in 1941, who consolidated his power in 1953, taking control of the military and dismissing parliament. He then began a massive overhaul of Iranian society, emphasizing secularism, the liberation of women, and economic development.

His policies toward Jews were supportive. After the Israeli War of Independence, Iran was the place people went to escape from Iraq. Yet despite the shah's public support of Israel and the Persian Jewish community, the people of Iran remained deeply anti-Semitic.

Lina Zargar Samimy (above) was born in Tehran in 1938. As a girl at school, she was called *najes*—as she explains, "that means dirty; the Jewish people were always called *najes*, that means somebody that you cannot touch, somebody who is going to make you dirty if you touch them."

To protect themselves, the family lived as crypto-Jews: pretending, except among themselves, that they were not Jews. This required them to live in extreme secrecy. Lina was not allowed to have any friends over for fear that the family would be exposed. She recalls her father's anger when her grandmother went out

Lina Samimy (*second from left*) with her family, including her grandmother wearing a chador, 1946
Courtesy of Lina Samimy

to shop at a kosher butcher. She went out wearing a chador to disguise herself. Her father flew into a rage. He lectured his mother: "Do you know how dangerous it is for our family if someone finds out that we are Jewish? You cannot do that!"

The father had recurring nightmares, Samimy recalls, of "the whole population of women wearing black chadors and a little boy running with them as they all throw stones at the Jews." The stress and pressure of leading secret lives eventually became so great that Samimy left Tehran in 1954 and spent two years studying in France before returning.

Zaki Ghavitian was born in Isfahan, Iran, in 1951. He encountered the same widespread anti-Semitism. "During Passover, we had a special kitchen. Matzah was made on a large stone in a fire in the courtyard. We had to be very careful. Muslims lived in the neighborhood and thought we were making matzah with the blood of Muslim children. I remember the two times they came and searched the house. I was six years old. I was trembling. You could not go to the police and say, 'Come, help.'"

During the Six-Day War, Ghavitian remembers, "the news reported 'Israel is destroyed.' The Muslims were very happy and handed out candy. No Jew had the courage to go out on the street, fearing they would be beaten. Three days later, the news was different. Now we feared even more to go out in the street. Revenge was in the air. The head of the Jewish community went to see the shah and said that the Jewish community was in danger. We need protection. The government was very good. They sent police to protect us." Nevertheless, Ghavitian left Iran after he graduated high school and moved to Montreal.

◀ Revolutionaries burn
a portrait of Shah
Mohammad Reza Pahlavi
in Tehran, during the
Iranian Revolution,
February 1978.
Photo: Michel Setboun /
Gamma-Rapho via Getty Images

◀ Ayatollah Khomeini waves
to crowds after returning
to Iran during the Iranian
Revolution, February 1979.
Photo: Alain Dejean / Sygma
via Getty Images

The shah's protection of the Jews was not to last. His regime became increasingly authoritarian. Opposition parties were marginalized or outlawed. Political and social protests were met with repression, illegal detention, and torture. When his economic reforms began failing in the 1970s, popular discontent boiled over.

In early 1978, massive demonstrations began against the shah's rule. Students, workers, secular intellectuals, and the Shi'i ulama (the Shia religious scholars led by Ayatollah Khomeini) joined forces and took to the streets. They were met by the police with bullets. Many people were killed by government forces, which led to larger demonstrations and more killings.

Finally, in January of 1979, the shah left the country. In April, Ayatollah Khomeini declared Iran an Islamic republic and proceeded to establish an extremely strict and conservative regime. Left-wing and moderate voices were suppressed. Women's rights were rolled back. Dress codes were established. Iran's official tolerance of its Jews and Israel changed to resemble the prevailing hostile sentiment in the rest of the Muslim world.

In 1980, Ghavitian returned to Iran. He did so fearfully. He describes the lengths he had to go to in order to enter the country.

> After the revolution, I went back to Iran to visit my parents that I had not seen in ten years and to get married. I was smuggled into the country by some Iranian friends who had a carpet business in Germany... I was very nervous. My friends brought some Scotch, made me drink it, and then rolled me in a carpet. They were friends with some guards and bribed them to let me in... Two days later we arrived in Tehran. I went straight to my sister's house. She began inviting Jewish families with marrying-age girls to the house. One girl attracted me. She said okay. I left Iran [rolled in a carpet again], waiting for her to escape to Israel so I could marry her.

Before the creation of the Islamic republic, there were 90,000 Jews in Iran. Now there are less than 15,000, most of whom are elderly and poor. Iran was the last Middle Eastern country to see a major exodus of Jews. In ten years' time, there will likely be almost no Jews left.

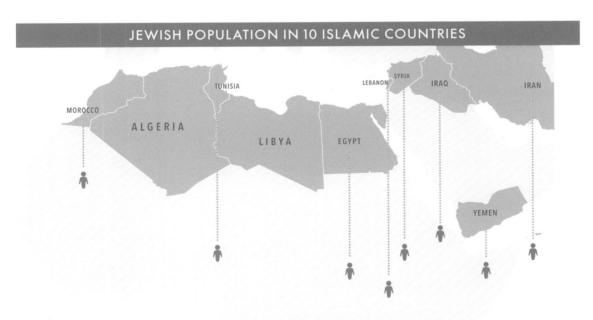

JEWISH POPULATION IN 10 ISLAMIC COUNTRIES

MOROCCO TUNISIA LEBANON SYRIA IRAQ IRAN

ALGERIA LIBYA EGYPT YEMEN

2020: 14,500

Source: sephardivoices.com

TODAY AND TOMORROW

"I'm from Baghdad.
The Arabic culture is part of me,
even today in Israel."

ELI AMIR

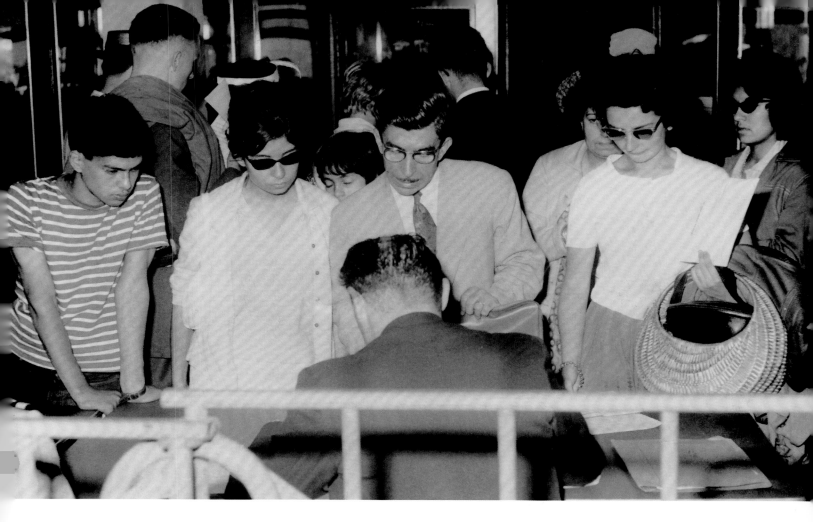

5 **IN JUST ONE GENERATION,** Jewish communities that had survived for thousands of years vanished. The Jews who remained struggled to survive in their ancient homelands. Of those who escaped, most left with nothing, forcing them to rebuild their lives in strange new lands. In Iraq, Egypt, and Morocco, Jews forfeited 100,000 square kilometers of land, an area five times larger than Israel. The businesses, houses, farms, bank accounts, and other assets that were left behind were worth today's equivalent of more than $100 billion (U.S.), roughly the size of the economies of Yemen, Iraq, and Tunisia combined. There have never been any reparations.

FINDING A NEW HOME

After the War of Independence, many of the displaced Sephardi fled to Israel. Despite efforts by the Jewish world to help, the response of the largely Ashkenazi population of Israel to the new citizens was often hampered by ignorance and prejudice. At times Eurocentric and patronizing, there was little recognition by

▲▲ Jakob Yusef, age seventy, and
niece Khalda Salih, thirty-
eight, members of the tiny
remaining Baghdad Jewish
community of roughly sixty
people, stand in their home
during Passover, 2003.
Photo: Mario Tama / Getty Images

▲ Albert Memmi, 1982
Photo: Claude Truong-Ngoc / Wikimedia Commons

the Ashkenazi of Sephardi identity, language (Arabic), and customs. The differences created not just barriers to understanding and acceptance, but often
outright hostility and discrimination. Assimilation into Ashkenazi culture, on
the other hand, meant the disappearance of Sephardi landmarks, common refer-
ences, languages (such as Haketia and Ladino), and cultural traditions including
food, music, and dance. Shared consciousness of communities evaporated.

Albert Memmi, a Sephardi displaced from Tunisia in the 1950s, describes his
trauma as follows: "I am ill at ease in my own land and I know of no other. My culture is borrowed, and I speak my mother tongue haltingly. I have neither religious
beliefs nor tradition ... to try to explain what I am, I would need much time ... I
am Tunisian but Jewish, which means I am politically and socially an outcast."[13]

In some cases the Sephardi Jews never recovered from the dispossession
and dislocation, but in others, extraordinary opportunities opened up for them
and their children. Whether in Canada, the U.K., Israel, France, Italy, or the
United States, many went on to prosper, making important contributions to their
adopted countries in business, science, and the arts. They enriched their new
nations—sometimes after much struggle.

At Israel's birth in 1948, the country had a population of just over 800,000,
including 650,000 Jews. By 1951, Israel had absorbed almost 600,000 more people. The Jews who went to Israel were part of an enormous wave of refugees that

Robert Khalifa's *laissez-passer*, a one-way visa allowing him to leave Egypt in 1963

included not only the Arab Jews, but hundreds of thousands of Holocaust survivors and displaced persons. Housing, feeding, and settling such an enormous number of refugees was a colossal undertaking for a small and poor country.

The problem was compounded by the vast cultural differences between the new arrivals and the Israelis, who were predominantly European Ashkenazi Jews. The Sephardi Jews did not speak the same language, they did not share the same customs and practices, and they did not have any resources at their disposal.

Eli Amir (p. 108), an Iraqi, describes the reception that the Sephardi received on arriving in Israel.

We were on one of the first flights and the flight was pretty scary. It was a primitive plane, it was shaking the whole time—I held my younger sister on my knees. My mom was pregnant and the kids cried during the flight because they were really scared of this box flying in the air. We got to Israel and then they kissed the ground and we were finally there.

The landing in Israel was a terrible time, because immediately we were called Arab Jews. Because we were fleeing from the Arabs, and now we are the Arabs. And they didn't understand anything about Arab culture, for them it was an enemy's culture that they beat in the war, and they didn't even teach people about us in school. We were nothing. We didn't exist on the Jewish

ELI AMIR
Born in Baghdad, Iraq, 1937
Arrived in Israel, 1951
Photo: David Blumenfeld

"We were called
Arab Jews . . .
We were nothing."

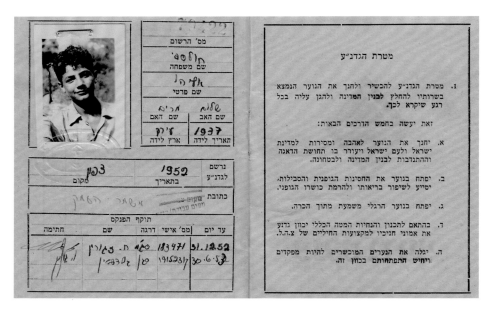

◀ Eli Amir's school
identity card from
1952, one year after
his arrival in Israel
Courtesy of Eli Amir

SHLOMO EL-KEVITY
Father left Iraq, 1951
Born in Israel, 1956
Photo: David Blumenfeld

"We were treated
like animals."

people's map and we became no ones. It was a feeling... every person came
with a self-appreciation, with last names that have histories, and all of a
sudden it was all over.

Amir's experience was typical. Shlomo El-Kevity (above) also came from an
artistically and intellectually sophisticated family. His father, Saleh Al Kuwaity,
is considered one of the founders of modern Iraqi music but left Iraq at the same
time as Eli Amir. Shlomo's parents didn't want to leave their successful lives
behind for Israel but felt they had no choice. On their arrival, the members of El-
Kevity's family, like Amir's, were "treated like animals," as El-Kevity described it:

They were all British educated, they all arrived with suits and ties in a British
style and when they arrived in Israel, it was claimed that they were bringing
diseases with them and they were sprayed with DDT, a substance against cock-
roaches. His hair was white, and it infuriated them.

I felt the pain this artist had, [who] left such a thing behind and became nothing here. A man, a Jew, who received a golden watch from the Iraqi king, and how he had to humiliate himself here.

The prejudice against the Sephardi in Israel was so great that babies of the Yemeni Jews were allowed to be taken from them and put up for adoption by Ashkenazi parents. The government felt that it would give the children a better future than anything they might receive from their own parents. It was only in 2021 that the government recognized this dreadful state of affairs, apologized for it, and agreed to pay reparations.

David Ben Gurion, the first prime minister of Israel, was very conscious of how badly treated the Sephardi were. In 1949, he deplored the fact that no Sephardi were appointed to the Supreme Court. He famously noted that "if there will be a government without a Sephardi or without a woman, that will be a flaw... Everyone needs to be in all our institutions."[14] The first Sephardi justice was not seated on the Supreme Court until 1962.

The challenge of absorbing the Sephardi was much easier for Canada, France, Italy, the U.K., and the U.S., since they were wealthier countries and there were far fewer refugees relative to the size of their populations. In the case of France, the displaced Jews from Morocco and Tunisia already spoke French, and the Algerians were already citizens. In all cases, the host countries created arrangements that allowed the new arrivals to integrate and pursue a path to full citizenship.

For the Gareh family, finding their place in Canada was simply a matter of making a few phone calls. Edna Gareh Mashaal (facing) says, "My father opened the telephone book when we came to Canada and wanted to see if there was another Iraqi in Montreal. My father was looking for other Iraqis and we started to meet some through other people and that's when we joined the Iraqi Club that my late father-in-law opened with another family."

The treatment of the displaced Sephardi was very different from the treatment of the Palestinians made homeless by the Israeli War of Independence. With the exception of Jordan, their Arab neighbors did not welcome the displaced Palestinians or grant them a path to citizenship. To the contrary, the policy of the Arab League was not to allow them in. The league forbade its members from offering citizenship; it preferred that the refugees live in camps in the parts of Palestine occupied by Jordan (West Bank) and Egypt (Gaza).

Although the displaced Jews and Palestinians were both declared refugees by United Nations Resolution 242, only the Palestinians were given assistance by the international community. The United Nations Relief and Works Agency (UNRWA) was created in 1948 primarily to assist the Palestinians. It is still in operation today and has a budget of roughly $600 million (U.S.) a year. The international community offered no comparable support to the Arab Jews.

EDNA GAREH MASHAAL
Born in Haifa, Israel, 1943
Arrived in Canada, 1959
Photo: Liam Sharp

"My father opened the telephone book when we came to Canada and wanted to see if there was another Iraqi in Montreal."

UNRWA defines a Palestinian refugee as someone whose home was in Mandatory Palestine before 1948, along with all their descendants on their father's side. There are now over five million registered Palestinian refugees, of whom more than 1.5 million are in official UNRWA refugee camps. UNRWA includes in this assessment Palestinians who are born in other countries and are citizens of that country, in contrast to all other refugees who must be first generation and displaced. The Palestinians are the oldest and, aside from the refugees of the Syrian Civil War, largest group of refugees in the world. There are no Sephardi refugee camps.

The Arab countries continue to demand the right for Palestinian refugees to return to their ancestral homes. They raise the matter continuously at the United Nations. In 1975, the Arab countries advocated for, and led the General Assembly to pass, a resolution (3379) declaring Zionism a form of racism. Since 1947, the UN has passed over eight hundred resolutions in total addressing the

Iraqi Jews at work in a *ma'abarot* (a refugee camp in Israel), 1951. The camps housed hundreds of thousands of mostly Mizrahi Jews before being dismantled in the early 1960s.
Photo: Teddy Brauner / Government Press Office (Israel)

Shlomo Hillel serves as Speaker of the Knesset, 1984
Courtesy of Shlomo Hillel

Yasser Arafat, chairman of the Palestine Liberation Organization (PLO), speaks to the United Nations General Assembly in New York, 1974.
Photo: Teddy Chen / UN Photo

Middle East and the conflict between Israel and the Arab nations—not a single one of which refers specifically to the nearly one million Jews who were displaced from Arab countries.

OF THE SEPHARDI who left, many built extraordinary careers in their new homes. In Israel, Shlomo Hillel, the intrepid organizer of the Ezra and Nehemiah airlift, went on to a distinguished political and diplomatic career. He became a member of the Knesset in 1952, later becoming Israeli ambassador to large swaths of Africa and a member of the delegation to the United Nations. He returned to the

Knesset in 1969, serving first as minister of police and then minister of the interior. He concluded his political career when he was elected speaker of the Knesset.

Eli Amir also went on to a distinguished career in Israel, becoming one of its most celebrated and successful writers. He did so while remaining true to his Babylonian roots. His best-known book, *The Dove Flyer*, later made into a film, is set in the Baghdad of his youth. He tells a lovely story about meeting one of Egypt's most distinguished playwrights, who was surprised that an Israeli could speak fluent Arabic. "It astonished him. And I told him . . . I'm from Baghdad. The Arabic culture is part of me, even today in Israel." It appears that even Egypt's most celebrated intellectuals did not seem to know that there were 850,000 Arab Jews.

Amir bemoans the collective forgetting of Arabs in Israel. He argues that it has been a "wasted opportunity" for the country not to have integrated Arab culture and language into social and political life. The failure to do so, he feels, has compounded Israel's problems with its neighbors. He notes that none of Israel's leaders have spoken Arabic: "The Israelis don't know Arabic. Prime Minister Ben-Gurion was a great man. He learned Spanish to read *Don Quixote*. Arabic he didn't learn. Did Golda know Arabic? Did Begin know Arabic? Shamir? Netanyahu? . . . They [the Arabs] are the majority around here. The minimum we can do is learn their language and culture."

A publicity photo of Mary Josielewski during her career as a professional singer, 1962
Courtesy of Mary Josielewski

For her part, Mary Judah-Jacob Josielewski, the little girl who saw her brother and mother killed during a pogrom in Yemen, ended up in a displaced persons camp in the city of Netanya, Israel. The conditions were so awful that she ran away at the age of twelve, ultimately being taken in by a relative in Tel Aviv. She finished high school, trained as a secretary, and started taking singing lessons. She became so good that she turned professional, performing first in Israel, later in London and New York. While in Manhattan, she met her husband, a Jewish real estate tycoon, ultimately joining him in the business and running it. The little Arabic-speaking orphan who was forbidden from photographing her own mother on the Magic Carpet airlift eventually had a son and three grandchildren. More than sixty years after leaving Yemen, she says she "preserves the heritage of my father's house. I am a Jew."

After Naim Dangoor lost his Iraqi citizenship and property, he settled permanently in London, with his wife Renée, the beauty queen, and his sons. There, he began again, creating a commercial property company. It did so well that in 1980, he established a charitable foundation to provide scholarships and financial support to disadvantaged youth. It was called the Exilarch's Foundation,

after the 1,100-year line of exilarchs (*rashei galuta*) of royal descent who headed and ruled the Jewish community in the area of Babylon. Naim Dangoor was knighted at age 101, the second-oldest man ever to be so honored.

The family remains one of the most generous in the United Kingdom. Naim's son, David, has continued Naim's work, running both the family business and the Exilarch's Foundation. He has made charitable donations to a multitude of educational organizations, including Imperial College (his alma mater), the Open University, Bar Ilan University, the Weizmann Institute, the UK Space Design Competition, and dozens more. Despite the Iraqi government's treatment of his family, David continues to work to preserve the history and culture of the Babylonian Jews. He says that "Iraq is still in our blood, in our bones. It is like a distant bell ringing in the back of our heads, always reminding us where we came from."

David Shama, the little boy who was given a puppy by King Farouk and whose father was sentenced to death, ended up in Montreal. He built up significant knitting and children's clothing businesses. When he retired, he decided to devote himself to his life's passion: dogs. He set up the Doghouse in Toronto as a daycare, kennel, and trainer. His particular focus is the rehabilitation of aggressive dogs. He is known there as the Dogfather.

Edwin Shuker, who had to disguise himself as a Christian for the entire time that he was at university, graduated, went to work, established a real estate company in London, and went on to significant financial success. Like David Dangoor, he is still haunted by his Babylonian heritage. In a remarkable return, he went back to Baghdad and sought out the house that he had lived in as a boy, the house where he spent his last hours "looking at all my collections, one at a time, saying goodbye to them" before the terrifying escape to Iran. More remarkably still, in 2019 he bought a house in Iraq, in Erbil in the Kurdish territories. He felt that he had to return. He says, "We are part and parcel of Iraq and I will not let go. I feel as if I'm a Jew living in Baghdad forever."

Elisa Diaine Scemama (facing), the daughter of Charles Diaine, who escaped from Algeria to France, enjoyed a career as a dentist. But despite France having the largest Sephardi population in the world outside of Israel, and one of the

ELISA DIAINE SCEMAMA
Father arrived in France, 1961
Born in Lyon, France, 1966
Arrived in the United States, 2000
Photo: Vincent Devries

"The skinheads
were shouting 'Jews
to the oven, Jews
out of France.'"

most successful, she feels that anti-Semitism is on the rise and that it is becoming dangerous for the Jews there. "So it's not politically correct to say there are places in the suburbs of Paris and even some places in Paris where you can't go if you're Jewish ... I had young guys telling me that I was a whore, a dirty Jew whore ... [At an anti-Israel demonstration], the extreme right and the skinheads were shouting 'Jews to the oven, Jews out of France.'" She finally left France and moved to the United States.

Jimmy Benaudis, who left Morocco after he finished high school and emigrated to France, expressed the same reservations. "The Second Intifada [2000] changed everything ... The mood started to change and I started feeling the same thing I was feeling in Morocco, like this is not my place ... The extreme right are not our friends, the extreme left are not our friends, the growing environmental movement are not our friends, the socialists are not our friends. So who is going to be on our side if anti-Semitism comes, and it will come ... And I don't want to face what I faced in Morocco. So we decided just to leave." Benaudis left with his family and moved to the United States. He established a successful career as a financial consultant and now is part of the large Sephardi community in Miami.

Despite such concerns about rising French anti-Semitism, many other Sephardi have made extraordinary contributions to France. Claude Cohen-Tannoudji's (left) family had lived in North Africa for hundreds of years, first in Tunisia and then in Algeria, where he was born and went to school. He moved to Paris for his university education and became a professor at the Collège de France, also lecturing at Harvard and MIT. In 1997, he was awarded the Nobel Prize in Physics.

His student, Serge Haroche, was born in Casablanca, Morocco. His parents and grandparents were students and taught at the Alliance Israélite Universelle schools. His family moved to France when he was ten. He currently holds the chair in quantum physics at the Collège de France. He was awarded the Nobel Prize in Physics in 2012.

Bernard-Henri Lévy, a distinguished public intellectual in France, was born in Algeria. He was one of the founders of the New Philosophers school, and is an author of many influential nonfiction works, a documentary filmmaker, a political activist, and an art curator. It is difficult to overstate his centrality to French intellectual and cultural life.

So too was Jacques Derrida, the most influential figure in the development of post-structuralism and postmodernism. He was also born in Algeria, but had to interrupt his education when he was expelled from his school by the Vichy government for being Jewish. By the end of his life, he had had a significant influence on all the humanities and social sciences. He was one of the foremost intellectual figures of the twentieth century.

Philosopher Jacques Derrida came from a Jewish family in Algeria and moved to Paris as a teenager.
Photo: Ulf Andersen / Getty Images

René Samuel Cassin was born to a Sephardi family in France. He was one of the drafters of the Universal Declaration of Human Rights for the United Nations, along with Eleanor Roosevelt and John Peters Humphrey, a Canadian. He was awarded the Nobel Peace Prize. He also became president of the Alliance Israélite Universelle, which had done so much to educate the children of the Arab Jews.

In Israel, too, the Sephardi refugees have made outstanding contributions. Apart from Shlomo Hillel and Eli Amir, Israel Kessar, who left Yemen as a young man, became head of the trade union movement. Ten Israeli Supreme Court judges and forty in the lower courts have been of Iraqi descent. Foreign ministers David Levy and Shlomo Ben-Ami came from Morocco.

Danny Ayalon (page 118), whose father left Algeria in 1947 because "he couldn't stand the discrimination against the Jews," grew up unaware of the forced exile of his family. "In our home, we never spoke about Algeria or the plight of Jews in the Arab countries." It was only after his parents were asked by his children about their history that he began to understand his own roots.

He sees in his father's unwillingness to talk about his past a parallel to many Holocaust survivors' difficulty speaking about theirs. "I see a lot of similarities in a psychological way, in a mental way between Holocaust survivors ... and the survivors of the Jewish expulsion from Arab countries following 1948, yes. There is an unexplainable factor here of shame, and maybe shame because they were helpless, they were not owning their own destiny. This is something we all have to understand and to strengthen them by encouraging them to tell their stories. In my mind, they are all heroes."

"They [the Sephardi]
are all heroes."

Ayalon had a distinguished political career as deputy foreign minister, ambassador to the United States, and member of the Knesset. "So I used my leadership capacity in the ministry to bring up the story of Jewish refugees, not only to the Israeli public but also to the international community... I also used my political power at the time to make sure the Israeli government will recognize the plight of the Jews from Arab countries by designating a day in the calendar which will honor them and the tragedies they suffered."

Ayalon helped bring about the creation of Yom Plittim, an annual memorial day on November 30, to recognize the plight of the Jews displaced from Arab lands, and as a celebration of their heritage.

Outside of Israel, many other Arab Jews made profound contributions to science, business and the arts.

André Aciman, the "dog of the Arabs," left Alexandria when he was a teenager and ended up in the United States. He is a novelist, essayist, and short story writer. His best-known work, *Call Me By Your Name*, was made into a very successful film and won the Lambda Literary Award for gay fiction in 2008.

Aldo Bensadoun was born in Morocco, but went to the United States and Canada for his university studies. In 1974, he founded the Aldo Group in Montreal, a massive footwear designer, manufacturer, and distributor, with nearly 300 stores across 100 countries.

In a similar vein, Paul Marciano was also born in Morocco. His father, grandfather, and great-grandfather were all rabbis. In 1981, he, along with his brothers, established Guess Jeans, which ultimately became Guess, the clothing and fashion company that designs and sells everything from shoes and swimwear to sunglasses and watches. It has an annual turnover of almost $2.5 billion (U.S.).

Gisèle Halimi was born in Tunisia in 1927 and emigrated to France. There she became one of the country's most distinguished human rights lawyers. She was also an early feminist and an advocate for women's right to reproductive choice. She chaired the tribunal that was set up by Bertrand Russell and Jean-Paul Sartre to examine American war crimes in Vietnam.

Tunisian Jew Gisèle Halimi (*left*), seen here with the actress Delphine Seyrig at the 1972 Bobigny abortion trial, immigrated to Paris in her twenties.
Photo: Michel Clement / AFP via Getty Images

▲ Jewish boxer Alphonse
Halimi, shown winning the
European bantamweight
champion title in October
1960, left Algeria for
France.
Keystone / Hulton Archive /
Getty Images

▲▶ Pfizer CEO Albert Bourla,
a Sephardi Jew from
Greece, on Capitol Hill
in Washington, DC,
February 2019
Photo: Zach Gibson / Bloomberg
via Getty Images

David Nahmad left Lebanon (though he is of Syrian extraction) and became one of the most important art dealers in the world. He bought and sold Picasso, Juan Gris, Georges Braque, Modigliani, all of the great European painters of the twentieth century. He is estimated to be worth $2 billion (U.S.) and resides in Monaco. Alphonse Halimi left Algeria and became the world bantamweight boxing champion. His nickname was La Petite Terreur (the Little Terror). More recently, Albert Bourla, a Sephardi Jew, is CEO of the Pfizer corporation—the first pharmaceutical company to have a Covid-19 vaccine approved by the U.S. Food and Drug Administration.

THE HOMES LEFT BEHIND

Despite these stories of success, the exodus of the Sephardi Jews from North Africa and the Middle East imposed a devastating cost on hundreds of thousands of people—but perhaps more importantly, it was also a catastrophe for the countries they left behind.

In Iraq, a significant proportion of the population of Baghdad had been Jewish. They were such a presence in daily life that, as Dhiaa Kasim Kashi, a Muslim, recalls, "business across the country used to shut down on Saturday because it was Jewish Shabbat. They were the most prominent members of every elite profession—bankers, doctors, lawyers, professors, engineers," as well as "all of Iraq's famous musicians and composers... The country suffered a big shock when the Jews left."[15] It is difficult to imagine any country being able to sustain the loss of so many of its best educated and most successful citizens.

The same was true of Egypt, where the Jewish community was central to its banking, commercial, and industrial life. As in Iraq, the purging of its economic elite badly hampered its future development. The country still suffers today from tepid growth and dreadful levels of unemployment. Egypt, like Iraq, is a poor country.

The loss of these gifted people, these scientists, businessmen, politicians, and intellectuals, inevitably produced a terrible hole in the social, cultural, and economic life of Ishmael's house. Would the last seventy years have been different if they had stayed and been allowed full citizenship and human rights?

Dhiaa Kasim Kashi, a Muslim, was born in Baghdad, Iraq, and arrived in England in 1980.
Photo: Liam Sharp

It is impossible to say, but Victor Mashaal believes their fate would have been very different. "What would Iraq be like today if there was no problem with the Jews? It would have been one of the wealthiest countries in the world. What is it now? Fifty million people, each one at the throat of the other, daily suicide bombings... And yet... and yet... All my grandchildren love Iraqi food. They come for Shabbat dinner and they always want Iraqi food. They join me for services conducted in a Sephardi way. They know they are Sephardi."

In some Arab countries, attempts are being made to make amends for the terrible treatment of Jewish citizens. Morocco is, so far, the outstanding example. Jewish community offices exist in several Moroccan cities; King Mohammed VI appointed a Moroccan Jew in 2006 as an ambassador-at-large, tasked with aiding the Middle East peace process; and the king retains another Moroccan Jew as a senior adviser. The old Jewish quarter of Fez, the Mellah, has become an object of both national and tourist acclaim. The synagogue was restored with UNESCO funds and a small museum was built in the old Jewish cemetery. Morocco established diplomatic relations with Israel and has begun teaching the history of the Holocaust in schools. The king has personally paid for the restoration of the Jewish cemeteries.

Saleh Al Kuwaity (*bottom center*), father of Shlomo El-Kevity (see page 109), is considered the founder of modern Iraqi music. In 1936, the king of Iraq's radio station began transmitting live music broadcasts three times a week. The brothers Saleh and Daoud (*bottom left*) formed a small orchestra with five other Jewish players, and soon began recording and performing across the country.

Courtesy of Shlomo El-Kevity

The restoration of synagogues has also been undertaken in Egypt, but with very strange results. Maimonides Synagogue in Cairo was renovated in part by the Egyptian government, which agreed to protect the Jewish cemetery and Maimonides's original yeshiva in the old city as well. But the synagogue remains locked and unused. Visitors require special permission to enter. It is a Potemkin synagogue: it looks beautiful, but it is empty.

A similar fate befell the restoration of the main synagogue in Alexandria. It was originally built in 1354, destroyed by Napoleon's bombardment of the port, and rebuilt in 1850. It seats 700 people. Like the synagogue in Cairo, its restoration was paid for by the government, which organized a formal reopening ceremony in January of 2020. Two hundred Egyptian Jews flew in from around the world to pray and participate. But nobody else came; there were no press releases and no press. Alec Nacamulli, originally from Egypt, was present for the ceremony. He noted that "it was as though the Egyptian government did not want its citizens to know the synagogue had been restored; the restoration was purely for foreign consumption."

The government of Egypt is clearly ambivalent about its relationship to its historic Jewish communities. On the one hand, it spends money restoring and protecting parts of Egypt's Jewish heritage; on the other it continues to stonewall access to its Jewish records. More recently, however, it seems to be starting to change. The ministry of education announced a new school subject called Common Values. The course is based on the verses and teachings that are common to

The Ben Ezra Synagogue in
Cairo, 2017
Photo: David Langer

the three great Abrahamic religions: Christianity, Islam, and Judaism. For the
first time ever, Egyptian students will be able to study Jewish texts. The government says that it reflects its desire to spread the values of tolerance and fraternity.

The government of Iraq also seems ambivalent. After the U.S. invasion in
2003, the American army found hundreds of Jewish documents—biblical scrolls,
identity cards, school reports, prayer books, fragments of Torahs—in the basement of Saddam Hussein's intelligence headquarters. They were badly water
damaged. The American government had them shipped to the U.S. National
Archives, which restored and preserved them as best they could.

Some of the Torahs, however, were so badly damaged that they could not be
restored and had to be buried. A burial service was organized by the Iraqi Jewish
community at the Montefiore Cemetery, ironically named New Babylon, on Long
Island. The ruined Torahs were buried following the same memorial service that
would be performed for a human. The rabbis presided and the Torahs were placed
in a coffin and lowered into the grave; the mourners took turns shoveling earth
on to the coffin to close the site.

The ownership of the documents remains the subject of considerable dispute.
The Iraqi government claimed them, as did the World Organization of Jews from
Iraq, and said they were part of Iraq's history and heritage. At the burial ceremony,
the Iraqi ambassador to the U.S. said that the new government of Iraq "would like
to preserve and cherish that history." Despite the ambassador's promise, the Iraqi
government has done nothing to make amends.

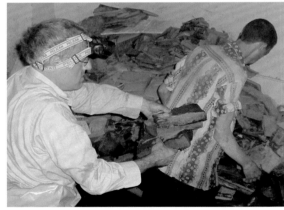

The Eliyahu Hanavi Synagogue in Alexandria reopened on January 10, 2020, three years after the Egyptian government started renovations. The synagogue was originally built in 1354.
Courtesy of Association Internationale, Nebi Daniel

◄ In 2003, U.S. army troops found tens of thousands of Jewish prayer books and documents in the basement of Saddam Hussein's intelligence headquarters.
Photo: Harold Rhode

▲ The damaged Torah scrolls were given a burial ceremony in the Montefiore Cemetery, by the local Iraqi Jewish community, 2013.
Photo: David Langer / Sephardi Voices

"Hear of Israel, learn the statutes I gave you... obey my covenant... The Lord made the covenant with us."
DEUTERONOMY 5:1–5

Damaged Torah scroll recovered from Baghdad, Iraq, and buried in the New Montefiore Cemetery, Long Island, New York, 2003
Photo: Raphael Abada

The sad truth is that the Arab countries have never come to grips with their lamentable treatment of their own citizens. Unlike Germany addressing its Nazi past, Canada and its terrible policies toward Indigenous peoples, or South Africa and its history of apartheid, there has been no effort to pursue a policy of truth and reconciliation. No government has organized public efforts to get at the truth of what happened, inform its citizens, and make amends.

As Irwin Cotler, the distinguished human rights lawyer and former Canadian minister of justice, notes: "Let there be no doubt about it: where there is no remembrance, there is no truth; where there is no truth, there will be no justice; where there is no justice, there will be no reconciliation; and where there is no reconciliation, there will be no peace."[16]

Or, as Eli Weisel, the Holocaust survivor and writer, put it in his speech accepting the Nobel Peace Prize: "Without memory, our existence would be barren and opaque... It is memory that will save humanity... Hope without memory is like memory without hope."[17] It is time for the Arab countries to remember.

It is also time to celebrate the extreme tenacity of the Sephardi Jews, the people who gave the world the stories of creation, of Moses and the laws, of the Tower of Babel, of the teachings of Jesus and those of Muhammad. Without them, the modern Western world would be deprived of its formative myths and religions. There would be no monotheism, no Torah, no New Testament, and no Koran.

It is time to celebrate the Sephardi Jews overcoming their endless displacements, first to Babylon and more recently from their ancient homes in the Middle East, North Africa, and Iran. Many left with nothing, and yet they endured and prospered. Theirs is a story of persistence and courage in the face of terrible circumstances. They rose again and again. They lived 2,500 years without their own state. They have prevailed.

TOP TO BOTTOM: Tomas Lopez photographing Michéle Karsenti in his studio at the University of Miami, Florida

Liam Sharp with Simon Keslassy at the Schwartz/ Reisman Centre in Maple, Ontario

Liam Sharp shooting a portrait of ninety-four-year-old Naim Dallal at his home in Toronto, Ontario

SEPHARDI FACES

Sephardi Voices: The Untold Expulsion of Jews from Arab Lands is a book of memory and retrieval. It preserves these individuals' memories of being expelled from their homelands, and memories of the worlds they left behind. It is also a book of redemption. The expelled Jews left with nothing, fled to unknown countries, and rebuilt their lives, often with great success. Their departure was a terrible loss to the countries they left and a gift to their new homelands.

Sephardi Voices tells the stories of only a few of the 850,000 who were displaced. But each of the untold stories represents a complete life and a complete world. Among them are countless tales of tragedy and heroism.

The Portrait Gallery is a small reminder and gesture of respect to the many stories that do not appear in the book. It celebrates some of those in the Sephardi Voices archive who left their ancestral homes in Algeria, Tunisia, Libya, Syria, Lebanon, Yemen, Egypt, Iraq, Morocco, and Iran to make new homes in the United States, Great Britain, Canada, Italy, and Israel. Their stories can be found at sephardivoices.com.

PIERRE BENHAIM
Born in Oran, Algeria, 1949
Arrived in the United States, 2015
Photo: Tomas Lopez

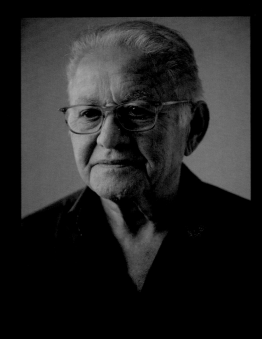

JULIEN AYACHE
Born in Algeria, 1937
Arrived in France, 1965
Photo: Michael Chavez

MICHÉLE HAGEGE KARSENTI
Born in Tunis, Tunisia, 1947
Arrived in the United States, 1985
Photo: Tomas Lopez

WALTER ARBIB
Born in Tunisia, 1941
Arrived in Canada, 1988
Photo: Liam Sharp

JOHN LASRY
Born in Tunis, Tunisia, 1943
Arrived in the United States, 1975
Photo: Tomas Lopez

NOEMI LIEBERMAN
Born in Tripoli, Libya, 1936
Arrived in Canada, 1957
Photo: Liam Sharp

ROSE OVADIA
Born in Aleppo, Syria, 1972
Arrived in the United States, 1987
Photo: Tomas Lopez

SHALOM YEFET
Born in Talabi, Yemen, 1947
Arrived in the United States, 1973
Photo: Tomas Lopez

MONICA ALEVY
Born in Cairo, Egypt, 1940
Arrived in the United States, 1999
Photo: Tomas Lopez

AVIVA MIZRAHI BEN HORIN
Born in Cairo, Egypt, 1952
Arrived in the United States, 1974
Photo: Tomas Lopez

BETTY BIVAS KANE
Born in Cairo, Egypt, 1944
Arrived in the United States, 1967
Photo: Tomas Lopez

LILIAN CARMONA GOZLAN
Born in Cairo, Egypt, 1924
Arrived in Canada, 1957
Photo: Liam Sharp

VIVIANNE SILVER
Born in Cairo, Egypt, 1942
Arrived in Canada, 1957
Photo: Liam Sharp

ALBERT LEVY
Born in Cairo, Egypt, 1934
Arrived in the United States, 2012
Photo: Tomas Lopez

ROLEN SABET
Born in Tehran, Iran, 1931
Arrived in the United States, 1953
Photo: Tomas Lopez

MOJDEH KHAGHAN DANIAL
Born in Tehran, Iran, 1967
Arrived in the United States, 1979
Photo: Tomas Lopez

ROBERT SIDI
Born in Beirut, Lebanon, 1951
Arrived in Canada, 1970
Photo: Liam Sharp

NINA RABIH HALLAK
Born in Beirut, Lebanon, 1942
Arrived in Canada, 1968
Photo: Alexandre Emond
Courtesy of Canadian Friends of Tel Aviv University, Montreal

ESTHER DIWAN
Born in Beirut, Lebanon, 1940
Arrived in Canada, 1970
Photo: Liam Sharp

ISAAC ABUHAV
Born in Beirut, Lebanon, 1959
Arrived in the United States, 1984
Photo: Tomas Lopez

RUTH MEIR
Born in Baghdad, Iraq, 1938
Arrived in Canada, 1966
Photo: Liam Sharp

NAIM DALLAL
Born in Baghdad, Iraq, 1924
Arrived in Canada, 1959
Photo: Liam Sharp

FLO DAHOUD URBACH
Born in Baghdad, Iraq, 1937
Arrived in Canada, 1964
Photo: Liam Sharp

HILLEL SHOHET
Born in Baghdad, Iraq, 1952
Arrived in the United States, 1981
Photo: Tomas Lopez

YEHESKEL KOJAMAN
Born in Baghdad, Iraq, 1920
Arrived in London, England, 1975
Photo: Liam Sharp

MAURICE SHOHET
Born in Baghdad, Iraq, 1949
Arrived in the United States, 1981
Photo: Liam Sharp

AIDA BASRI ZELOUF
Born in Baghdad, Iraq, 1953
Arrived in London, England, 1974
Photo: Liam Sharp

ODED HALAHMY
Born in Baghdad, Iraq, 1938
Arrived in the United States, 1970
Photo: Liam Sharp

CYNTHIA SHAMASH KAPLAN
Born in Baghdad, Iraq, 1963
Arrived in the United States, 1992
Photo: Liam Sharp

MIKE YUVAL
Born in Baghdad, 1939
Arrived in Canada, 1968
Photo: Liam Sharp

ROBERT MASHAAL
Born in Montreal, Canada, 1963
Photo: Liam Sharp

SASSOON SHAHMOON
Born in Jerusalem, Israel, 1934
Arrived in Canada, 1980
Photo: Liam Sharp

EDMOND ELBAZ
Born in Safi, Morocco, 1942
Arrived in Canada, 1968
Photo: Liam Sharp

SYLVAIN ABITBOL
Born in Casablanca, Morocco, 1949
Arrived in Canada, 1968
Photo: Liam Sharp

SIMON KESLASSY
Born in Tangier, Morocco, 1946
Arrived in Canada, 1972
Photo: Liam Sharp

CLAUDE BENARROCH
Born in Safi, Morocco, 1941
Arrived in Canada, 1968
Photo: Louis-Philippe Besner

BOB ORÉ ABITBOL
Born in Casablanca, Morocco, 1948
Arrived in Canada, 1965
Photo: Liam Sharp

SETE BENTATA DE BASSAN
Born in Tétouan, Morocco, 1959
Arrived in the United States, 2011
Photo: Tomas Lopez

YEHUDA BEN HORIN
Born in Wazan, Morocco, 1947
Arrived in the United States, 1974
Photo: Tomas Lopez

JOSEPH ZAGURY
Born in Safi, Morocco, 1943
Arrived in Canada, 1979
Photo: Jeff Ridout

ACKNOWLEDGMENTS

OVER THE LAST DECADE, many have contributed to the creation of a Sephardi Voices archive to remember and commemorate those displaced from North Africa, the Middle East, and Iran. The umbrella includes not only those displaced who have shared their stories, but also their children, grandchildren, and the human rights community. Numerous organizations including Sephardi organizations, educational institutions, rabbis, national and local leaders, advocates for social justice, and hundreds of individuals have donated their time and honor us with their voices. The Sephardi Voices project has spanned many countries including the United States, Canada, Mexico, the U.K., France, Italy, and Israel. Without their support, *Sephardi Voices: The Untold Expulsion of Jews from Arab Lands* would not have been possible.

Sephardi Voices volunteers have given their time to connect us with family and friends, to be trained to conduct interviews, and to help in the production of the interviews, the making of films, the creation of portrait exhibits, in conducting research, the writing of articles, zoom presentations, speaking at forums, and more. In a few cities, there are a handful who not only welcomed Sephardi Voices but served as our ambassadors and worker bees: Bea Lewkowicz, Lyn Julius, and Varda Aron in London; Lisette Shashoua, Gladys Moallem, and Nathalie Benarroch in Montreal; Flo Urbach and Noemi Lieberman in Toronto; Levana Zamir and Margalit Bejarano in Israel; David Gerbi in Rome; Charles and Gislaine Diaine in Paris; Stanley Urman, Cynthia Shamash Kaplan, and David Dangoor in New York; Lior Haiat, Yoram Millman, and Carol Kaplan in Miami; Maurice Shohet in Washington; and Sam Yebri and Jilla Yousefi in Los Angeles. We are grateful to each and every one who has taken our hands and walked with us along the path.

We are especially indebted to Professor Green's research assistants from the University of Miami: Elena Scemama, Giancarlo Atassi, Shannan Berzack, and Leslie Benaudis; and from Miami Dade College: Amalia Padron. Everyone was either an immigrant themselves or the child of an immigrant to Miami. They spoke the languages of those displaced: French, Hebrew, and Spanish. To our photographers, Liam Sharp, Tomas Lopez, and David Blumenfeld, and for all those who have spent countless hours managing and coordinating the project: in Canada, David Langer, Rachel Abitan, Michelle Devorah Kahn, Zoë Lepiano, and Rebecca Lash; in USA, Trevor Green and Kineret BenKnaan; and in Israel, Tamar Morad and Ruth Saragosti. And to our publisher, Figure 1, and everyone there: Lara Smith, Naomi MacDougall, Mike Leyne, Richard Nadeau, Pam Robertson, Renate Preuss, and Mark Redmayne.

The Sephardi Voices USA Board of Directors has helped the writing of this book mature from an idea to a reality. Michael Sabet, Elisa Diaine, and Juliette Glasser not only represent the displaced population but more importantly have enabled us to connect with the Sephardi community globally. A robust thanks to them and to Jillian Bandes, Jonathan Nelson, Beth Jacob Congregation, Flo Urbach, Trae Williamson, Dana Post Adler, Oded Halahmy, Hillel Shohet, and the Dallal family—in memory of Naim Dallal, who have made it possible to provide free copies of the book to Jewish educators and to those who are actively involved in sponsoring Yom Plittim events (Sephardi Refugee Day—November 30). In the months ahead, the Sephardi Voices archive will become accessible without cost at the National Library of Israel.

Finally, Sephardi Voices is deeply appreciative of David Dangoor OBE, in London, who has made this project viable. His vision and support not only strengthen the Sephardi and Iraqi Jewish heritage, but also *Klal Yisrael*, the Jewish community.

We invite you to celebrate and share these voices and the Sephardi and Mizrahi heritage.

HENRY GREEN
RICHARD STURSBERG

GLOSSARY

ALIYAH There were five main waves of Zionist immigration to Palestine, or *aliyot*, before the creation of the State of Israel in 1948. The first wave of Jewish immigrants from Russia, Romania, and Yemen came throughout the late nineteenth century. The Second Aliyah took place before World War I, consisting predominantly of Jews escaping anti-Semitism in Russia. The Third Aliyah took place between World War I and 1921, with Jews arriving from Europe after the Balfour Declaration. The Fourth Aliyah took place between 1924 and 1929, mostly of Jews from Eastern Europe, but some from Iraq and Yemen. Between 1929 and World War II, nearly 250,000 Jews emigrated to Mandate Palestine during the Fifth Aliyah.

ALIYAH BET Code name given to illegal Jewish immigration to Palestine.

ARAB JEWS Jews living in or originating from Arab countries in North Africa and the Middle East.

ASHKENAZI JEWS Jews originating from central and eastern Europe.

BA'ATH PARTY A socialist and anti-imperialist movement, founded in 1943, that supported pan-Arab nationalism and the establishment of a unified Arab state. Saddam Hussein in Iraq and the al-Assad family in Syria were members of the Ba'ath Party.

BABYLONIAN JEWS Jews originating from Iraq. Some Iraqi Jews prefer the term "Babylonian Jew" over "Arab Jew" because the community has existed since the exile of Jews from Judea to Babylonia in the sixth century BCE.

BLOOD LIBEL An anti-Semitic conspiracy theory common to medieval Europe in which Jews were accused using Christian blood, particularly of children, for ritual purposes.

CASBAH Literally, citadel, fortress; the residential quarter that surrounds it, especially in North Africa. The Casbah in Algiers is a well-known heritage site.

CHADOR A cloak worn by Muslim women leaving only the face exposed.

DHIMMI An Arabic term historically given to non-Muslim populations living in Islamic countries. The term literally means "protected persons." They were exempt from certain duties assigned specifically to Muslims and were restricted from certain privileges and freedoms reserved for Muslims.

FARHUD Or "violent dispossession," this was an anti-Jewish pogrom against Iraqi Jews that took place in Baghdad in June 1941.

FRONT DE LIBÉRATION NATIONALE (FLN) Nationalist movement during the Algerian war against French colonial occupation.

JIHAD Arabic word that literally means "struggle against the enemies of Islam"; spiritually it means struggle within oneself against sin.

JIZYA a historical tax paid by non-Muslim populations in Muslim states.

JUDAEO-ARABIC Dialects of Arabic spoken by Arab Jewish communities in the Middle East and North Africa.

KNESSET The Israeli legislature.

KOL NIDREI A Jewish prayer, in Aramaic, that begins the Yom Kippur service.

KOSHER Food that conforms to Jewish dietary regulations.

LADINO Also known as Judaeo-Spanish, Ladino is a dialect spoken by Sephardi Jews from North Africa, the Balkans, Turkey, and Mediterranean regions.

MATZAH Unleavened flatbread eaten during the days of the Jewish festival Passover.

MELLAH "The Jewish quarter"; the Mellah of Fez, Morroco, is a historic site.

MINHAG Customs.

MIZRAHI JEWS A blanket term given to Jews from Muslim countries in the early State of Israel.

MUSLIM BROTHERHOOD An Islamist organization founded by Hassan al-Banna in 1928. Al-Banna believed in Muslim religious revival as an anti-colonial and economic development strategy.

NAJES Ritually unclean; contact with *najes* things brings a Muslim into a state of ritual impurity.

NAKBA "The Catastrophe" in Arabic. The exodus of an estimated 725,000 Palestinians during the Israeli War of Independence in 1948.

PASSOVER A Jewish holiday that commemorates the biblical story of the Exodus and the liberation of the Jewish people from slavery in Egypt.

PERSIAN JEWS Jews who historically lived in the Persian Empire. Today identified as Iranian Jews.

PIEDS-NOIRS Meaning "Blackfeet," it is a term given to French colonists who were born or lived in Algeria during the period of French rule. They were also called *colons*.

SEPHARDI JEWS In this book, we use the terms "Sephardi" and "Mizrahi" to refer to Jews (other than Persian Jews) who share a common heritage, culture and language with their Arab neighbors (see page 3).

SHABBAT The sacred day of rest in Judaism, starting from sundown on Friday to sundown on Saturday. Observing Shabbat includes abstaining from work, attending prayer services, and gathering on Friday evening for a family meal.

SHAVUOT A Jewish holiday that commemorates the giving of the law, the Torah.

SHIA/SHIITE The second-largest branch of Islam (10 to 15 percent of the Muslim population worldwide). Iran is a majority Shia country.

SUNNI The largest branch of Islam (85 to 90 percent of the Muslim population worldwide).

UNRWA The United Nations Relief and Works Agency for Palestine Refugees in the Near East. UNRWA's mandate also included supporting Jewish refugees displaced during the war of 1948. The organization defined Palestine refugees as "persons whose normal place of residence was Palestine during the period 1 June 1946 to 15 May 1948, and who lost both home and means of livelihood as a result of the 1948 conflict."[18] UNRWA provides essential services such as education and humanitarian aid to Palestinian refugees in the Middle East today.

YOM KIPPUR The holiest day in the Jewish calendar. It takes place after Rosh Hashanah (the Jewish new year). Jews traditionally observe this holy day with a day-long fast to atone and repent.

YOM PLITTIM Memorial Day, November 30, which marks the displacement of Jews from Arab countries and Iran.

ZIONISM A nationalist movement originating in nineteenth-century Europe that supports Jewish national self-determination. Zionism spawned the kibbutz movement to settle agricultural land in Palestine. There are many different branches of political Zionism, including Labor Zionism, Revisionist Zionism, and Cultural Zionism. Religious Zionism that espouses a spiritual connection between Jews and the land of Israel predates political Zionism and is a core component of Jewish religion.

NOTES

1   Joseph Herman Hertz, ed., *The Pentateuch and Haftorahs* (London: Soncino Press, 1960), 58.

2   Unless otherwise specified, all quotes from scripture have been translated from the Tanakh by Henry Green.

3   Tim Mackintosh-Smith, *Arabs: A 3,000-Year History of Peoples, Tribes and Empires* (New Haven: Yale University Press, 2019), xvii.

4   Unless otherwise noted, quotes are from interviews conducted for Sephardi Voices, an audiovisual archive primarily hosted at sephardivoices.com.

5   Martin Gilbert, *In Ishmael's House: A History of Jews in Muslim Lands* (Toronto: McClelland and Stewart, 2010), 181.

6   Gilbert, *In Ishmael's House*, 181.

7   Gilbert, *In Ishmael's House*, 157.

8   Gilbert, *In Ishmael's House*, 262.

9   Gilbert, *In Ishmael's House*, 278.

10 Gilbert, *In Ishmael's House*, 293.

11 Gilbert, *In Ishmael's House*, 295.

12 Mustafa Tlass, *The Matzah of Zion* (self-pub, 1983). Cited in Gilbert, *In Ishmael's House*, 308.

13 Ilan Stavans, *The Schocken Book of Modern Sephardic Literature* (New York: Schocken Books, 2005), xvii.

14 Gidi Weitz and Yechiam Weitz, "In the Whole Sephardi Community There Is No Worthy Candidate for the Supreme Court," *Ha'aretz*, January 22, 2021, 12.

15 Tamar Morad, Dennis Shasha, and Robert Shasha, eds., *Iraq's Last Jews: Stories of Daily Life, Upheaval, and Escape from Modern Babylon* (New York: Palgrave Macmillan, 2008), 202.

16 Irwin Cotler, David Matas, and Stanley Urman, "Jewish Refugees from Arab Countries," unpublished paper produced by Justice for Jews from Arab Countries (JJAC), 1.

17 Elie Wiesel, "Hope, Despair and Memory," Nobel lecture, December 11, 1986, www.nobelprize.org/prizes/peace/1986/wiesel/lecture/.

18 UNRWA, "Who Are Palestine Refugees?" https://www.unrwa.org/palestine-refugees.

RECOMMENDED READINGS, MEDIA, AND MUSEUMS

The following list provides a brief overview of resources on the history, culture, and refugee experience of Arab/Sephardi/Mizrahi Jews that have been helpful in the writing of this book. Opinions expressed in these resources do not necessarily represent the views of Sephardi Voices.

BOOKS AND PERIODICALS

Aciman, André. *Out of Egypt.* New York: Macmillan, 2007.

Adogame, Afe, Raimundo Baretto, and Wanderley Perreira da Rosa, eds. *Migration and Public Discourse in World Christianity.* Minneapolis: Augsburg Fortress, 2019.

Aharoni, Reuben. *The Jews of the British Crown Colony of Aden: History, Culture, and Ethnic Relations.* Leiden: Brill Publishers, 1994.

Azses, Hayim. *The Shoah in the Sephardic Communities: Dreams, Dilemmas, and Decisions of Sephardic Leaders.* Sephardic Educational Center in Jerusalem, 2005.

Bahloul, Joëlle. *The Architecture of Memory: A Jewish-Muslim Household in Colonial Algeria 1937–1962.* Cambridge University Press, 1996.

Bashkin, Orit. *Impossible Exodus: Iraqi Jews in Israel.* Stanford University Press, 2017.

Bashkin, Orit. *New Babylonians: A History of Jews in Modern Iraq.* Stanford University Press, 2012.

Basri, Carole. "The Jewish Refugees from Arab Countries: An Examination of Legal Rights—A Case Study of the Human Rights Violations of Iraqi Jews." *Fordham International Law Journal*, Vol. 26, Issue 3, 2002, 656–720.

Beinin, Joel. *The Dispersion of Egyptian Jewry: Culture, Politics and the Formation of a Modern Diaspora.* Oakland: University of California Press, 1998.

Ben-Nun Benayoun, Robert. *Looking for Home: Memoirs of a Sephardi Jew from Morocco.* Austin: Positive Imaging, LLC, 2020.

Ben-Porat, Mordechai. *To Baghdad and Back: The Miraculous 2,000 Year Homecoming of the Iraqi Jews.* New York: Gefen Publishing House, 1998.

Bensoussan, Georges. *Les Juifs du monde arabe: La question interdite.* Paris: Odile Jacob, 2017.

Boum, Aomar, and Sarah Abrevaya Stein, eds. *The Holocaust and North Africa.* Stanford University Press, 2019.

Cohen, Yolande. *Les Sépharades du Québec: Parcours d'exils nord-africains.* Montreal: Del Busso Editeur, 2017.

Cotler, Irwin, David Matas, and Stanley Urman. "Jewish Refugees from Arab Countries: The Case for Rights and Redress." *Justice for Jews from Arab Countries*, November 5, 2007.

Fischbach, Michael. *Jewish Property Claims against Arab Countries.* New York: Columbia University Press, 2008.

Gerber, S. Jane. *Cities of Splendour in the Shaping of Sephardi History.* Liverpool: The Littman Library of Jewish Civilization, 2020.

Gilbert, Martin. *In Ishmael's House: A History of Jews in Muslim Lands.* Toronto: McClelland and Stewart, 2010.

Gilbert, Martin. *The Jews of Arab Lands: Their History in Maps.* London: World Organization of Jews from Arab Countries, 1976.

Julius, Lyn. *Uprooted: How 3000 Years of Jewish Civilization in the Arab World Vanished Overnight.* Borehamwood, U.K.: Vallentine Mitchell Publishers, 2018.

Kalmar, Ivan Davidson, and Derek Jonathan Penslar. *Orientalism and the Jews.* University Press of New England, 2005.

Kattan, Naim. *Farewell, Babylon: Coming of Age in Jewish Baghdad.* Boston: David R. Godine, 2007.

Khazzoom, Loolwa, ed. *The Flying Camel: Essays on Identity by Women of North African and Middle Eastern Jewish Heritage.* Seattle: Seal Press, 2003.

Lagnado, Lucette. *The Man in the White Sharkskin Suit: A Jewish Family's Exodus from Old Cairo to the New World.* New York: HarperCollins, 2008.

Laskier, Michael. *The Alliance Israélite Universalle and the Jewish Communities of Morocco: 1862–1962.* State University of New York Press, 1983.

Laskier, Michael. *The Jews of Egypt, 1920–1970: In the Midst of Zionism, Anti-Semitism, and the Middle East Conflict.* New York University Press, 1991.

Laskier, Michael. *North African Jewry in the Twentieth Century: The Jews of Morocco, Tunisia, and Algeria.* New York University Press, 1997.

Levy, Isaac Jack. *And the World Stood Silent: Sephardic Poetry of the Holocaust.* Urbana and Chicago: University of Illinois Press, 1989.

Lewis, Bernard. *The Jews of Islam.* Princeton University Press, 1984.

Lichtenstein, Nina B. *Sephardic Women's Voices: Out of North Africa.* Santa Fe: Gaon Books, 2016.

Loeffler, James. *Rooted Cosmopolitans: Jews and Human Rights in the Twentieth Century.* Yale University Press, 2018.

Roumani, Maurice M. *The Case of the Jews from Arab Countries: A Neglected Issue.* Tel Aviv: World Organization of Jews from Arab Countries (WOJAC), 1983.

Setton, Ruth Knafo. *The Road to Fez.* Berkeley: Counterpoint Press, 2001.

Shohat, Ella. *On the Arab-Jew, Palestine, and Other Displacements: Selected Writings.* London: Pluto Press, 2017.

Somekh, Sasson. *Baghdad, Yesterday: The Making of an Arab Jew.* Jerusalem: Ibis Editions, 2007.

Stillman, Norman A. *The Jews of Arab Lands: A History and Source Book.* Philadelphia: The Jewish Publication Society of America, 1979.

Yerushalmi, Yosef Hayim. *Zakhor: Jewish History and Jewish Memory.* New York: Schocken Books, 1989.

FILMS

The Forgotten Refugees. Directed by Michael Grynszpan, 2006.
The Silent Exodus. Directed by Pierre Rehov, 2004.

SEPHARDI VOICES PRODUCTIONS

Last Class in Baghdad. Directed by David Langer, 2018.
A Story for Elina. Directed by David Langer, 2015.
What We Left Behind. Directed by David Langer, 2014.

FILMS BY COUNTRY

ALGERIA

In the Beginning: Once Upon a Time . . . There Were Arab Jews. Directed by Serge Lalou, 1997.

EGYPT

Jews of Egypt. Directed by Amir Ramses, 2013.

IRAN

Jews of Iran. Directed by Ramin Farahani, 2005.

IRAQ

The Dove Flyer. Directed by Nissim Dayan, 2014.

Forget Baghdad: Jews and Arabs—The Iraqi Connection. Directed by Samir, 2002.

Remember Baghdad. Directed by Fiona Murphy, 2017.

Saving the Iraqi Jewish Archives: A Journey of Identity. Directed by Carole Basri and Adriana Davis, 2020.

Shadow in Baghdad. Directed by Duki Dror and Galia Dror, 2013.

The Wolf of Baghdad. Directed by Carol Isaacs, 2020.

ISRAEL/PALESTINE

Ma'abarot. Directed by Dina Zvi-Riklis, 2019.

LEBANON

The Jews of Lebanon: Loyalty to Whom? Directed by Nada Abdelsamad, 2010.

LIBYA

The Last Jews of Libya. Directed by Vivienne Roumani-Denn, 2007.

Libya—The Last Exodus. Directed by Ruggero Gabbai, 2017.

MOROCCO

The Midnight Orchestra. Directed by Jérôme Cohen-Olivar, 2016.

Moroccan Jews. Destinies Undone. Directed by Younwa Laghrari, 2015.

Routes of Exile: A Moroccan Jewish Odyssey. Directed by Eugene Rosow, 1982.

They Were Promised the Sea. Directed by Kathy Wazana, 2013.

Tinghir-Jerusalem. Directed by Kamal Hachkar, 2014.

SYRIA

The Syrian Jewish Community: Coming to America (1900–1919). Directed by Lisa Ades, 2010.

The Syrian Jewish Community: Our Journey through History. Sephardic Heritage Museum, 2019.

TUNISIA

The Jews of Djerba. Directed by Alain Cohen and Georges Nizan, 1987.

Pillar of Salt. Directed by Haim Shiran, 1980.

YEMEN

About the Jews of Yemen. Directed by Johanna Spector, 1996.

MUSEUMS

EUROPE

Amussef: The Living Memory of Jewish Communities in the Sephardi, Mediterranean and Eastern World. www.amussef.org.

ISRAEL

Association of European Jewish Museums, Museum of Libyan Jews. www.aejm.org.

Babylonian Jewry Heritage Center. www.bjhcenglish.com.

International Association of Jews from Egypt. www.egyptian-jews.info/en.
Museum of Jews from Yemen and Israel Communities. www.bet-moreshet.co.il.
Museum of Yemenite Jewish Heritage. www.teman.org.il.
North Africa Jewish Heritage Center. www.mjc-jerusalem.com.

NORTH AMERICA
Sephardic Heritage Museum: International Center for Syrian Jewish Heritage,
    Preservation, and Education. www.sephardicheritagemuseum.com.

ORGANIZATIONS
The American Sephardi Federation. www.americansephardi.org.
Diarna: Mapping Mizrahi Heritage. www.diarna.org.
Federation CJA: The Communauté Sépharade Unifiée du Québec.
    https://100.federationcja.org/agencies/csuq.
Harif: Association of Jews from the Middle East and North Africa. www.harif.org.
Institut Sépharade Européen, Facebook Group. www.facebook.com/InstitutSef.
Jews Indigenous to the Middle East and North Africa. www.jimena.org.
Justice for Jews from Arab Countries. www.justiceforjews.com.
Sephardi Voices U.K. www.sephardivoices.org.uk
Sephardi Voices USA, Inc. www.sephardivoices.com.

COUNTRY-BASED ORGANIZATIONS
EGYPT
Association Internationale Nebi Daniel. www.nebidaniel.org.
Historical Society of the Jews from Egypt. www.hsje.org.
The International Association of Jews from Egypt. www.egyptian-jews.info.

IRAN
Iranian-American Jewish Federation of New York. www.iajfny.org.
30 Years After. www.30yearsafter.org.

IRAQ
Iraqi Jewish Association of Ontario. www.ijao.ca.

LEBANON
Lebanese Jewish Community Council, Facebook Group. www.facebook.com/
    BeirutSynagogue.

MOROCCO
Mimouna Association. www.mimouna.org.
UJA Federation of Greater Toronto. www.jewishtoronto.com/directory/
    communaute-juive-marocaine-de-toronto.

All URLs accessed April 28, 2021.

INDEX

Photographs and other illustrations indicated by page numbers in italics

Abehassera, Rouhama, *30*
Abehassera, Sarah, *30*
Abitbol, Bob Oré, *137*
Abitbol, Sylvain, *136*
Abouti, Joseph, 36–37, 68
Abraham, 7–8
Abuhav, Isaac, *132*
Aciman, André, *74, 74–75,* 118
Acre, Steve (Sabih Azra Ereb), 63, *63–64*
Aden, 22, 40, 53, 58, 60–61.
    See also Yemen
Ades, Lisette Shashoua, 27, *27, 93, 93*
Ades, Shafiq, 55, *55,* 66
Aldo Group, 119
Aleppo (Syria), 37, 54
Alevy, Monica, *130*
Alexander the Great, 11–12
Alexandria (Egypt), 12, 23, 122
Algeria: Algerian Revolution, 80–82, *82;* Crémieux Decree, 33, *33,* 78; exodus from, 82, *83;* French colonial rule and social/racial inequalities, 3, 15, 22, 33–34, 78–80; Great Synagogue (Synagogue de Rue Randon, Algiers), 34, *44;* Jewish population, 49, 68, 96, *103; L'Antijuif algérien* (newspaper), 34; photographs of Jews, *17, 33;* Roman Empire and, 12; WWII and, 43, 46
Alliance Israélite Universelle, 29, 33, 116, 117
Amir, Eli, 107, *108,* 109, 113
Arab, definition, 17
Arab countries: amends to Sephardi Jews, 121–23; First Arab–Israeli War (1948), 55, 56, 58; Jewish population, 49, 68, 96, *103;* against Jewish state, 51, 52, 53–54; lack of truth and reconciliation, 125; nationalism, 17, 19, 20, 22; Six-Day War, 86, *86,* 88–89, *89,* 95, 101; Yom Kippur War, 96–97, *97,* 98. *See also* Algeria; Egypt; Iran; Iraq; Lebanon; Libya; Morocco; Ottoman Empire; Palestinian Arabs; Syria; Tunisia; Yemen

Arab Jews, 3. *See also* Sephardi Jews
Arab League, 51, *52,* 53, 54, 55, 110
Arafat, Yasser, *112*
Arbib, Walter, *128*
Arch of Titus, *12*
Armistice Line (Green Line), *57*
Aron, Maria Meghnagi, 88, *88*
Ashkenazi Jews, 3, 105–6, 107, 110
al-Assad, Hafez, 97
Assyrians, *10*
Austria, 15
Ayache, Julien, *128*
Ayalon, Danny, 117–18, *118*
Azar, Samuel, 70
Azouli, Esther, *24*
Azouli, Joseph, *24*

Ba'ath Party (Iraq), 76–78, 89–91
Babylon, *11*
Babylonian captivity, 9, 11
Babylonian Jews, 3. *See also* Iraq
Baghdad (Iraq): British conquest of, 20, 25; destruction of Jewish cemetery, 76; Farhud (anti-Jewish pogrom), 47, *47–*49; impact of exodus, 121; Jewish population, 27, 28. *See also* Iraq
Baghdad Chamber of Commerce, 26
Balfour Declaration, 20, 22, *24,* 42
al-Banna, Hassan, 24, *24,* 69
Bar Kokhba revolt, 13
Barzani, Masoud, 92
Basri, Meir, *26*
Ben-Ami, Shlomo, 117
Benarroch, Claude, *136*
Benaudis, Jimmy, 85, *86,* 87, 98, *98,* 115
Ben Ezra Synagogue (Cairo, Egypt), 24, *123*
Benghazi (Libya), 35, 45
Ben Gurion, David, 110, 113
Benhaim, Pierre, *128*
Ben Horin, Aviva Mizrahi, *130*
Ben Horin, Yehuda, *137*
Bensadoun, Aldo, 119
Beth Alpha Synagogue (Israel), *8*
Black Saturday (Egypt), 69, 71
blood libel, 15, 98
Bourghiba, Habib, 75

Bourla, Albert, 120, *120*
Britain. *See* United Kingdom
Byzantine Empire, 13, 15

Cairo (Egypt), 23, 54, 69, 122
Camus, Albert, 81
Canada, 110, 114, 119
Cassin, René Samuel, 117
Cattaui Pasha, Joseph, 24
Christianity, 8, 12–13, 14–15
Churchill, Winston, 46
Cohen-Tannoudji, Claude, 116, *116*
"Copenhagen Maimonides" (manuscript), *14*
Cotler, Irwin, 125
Covenant of Omar, 14
Crémieux Decree, 33, *33,* 78
Crusades, 15
Cyrus the Great, 11

Dallal, Naim, *126, 133*
Dangoor, Abdullah, 48–49, *49,* 77
Dangoor, David, 114
Dangoor, Hakham Ezra, 26
Dangoor, Naim, *v, 49, 77, 77–*78, *78,* 113–14, *114*
Dangoor, Renée (née Dangor), *v, 77, 78,* 113
Dangoor family (Iraq), *77*
Danial, Mojdeh Khaghan, *131*
David (king of Israel), 8
De Bassan, Sete Bentata, *137*
De Gaulle, Charles, 81, *81*
Derrida, Jacques, 116, 117
dhimmi status, 14, 16, 19, 25, 29, 34, 40, 41
Diaine, Charles, *79,* 81, *81–*82
Diaine, Émile, *79, 79–*80
Diaine, Gislaine Levy, *80, 80–*81
Diwan, Esther, *132*
Dura-Europos Synagogue (Syria), *10*

Eban, Abba, *52*
École André Chénier (Morocco), *87*
École de l'Alliance Israélite (Tétouan, Morocco), *31*

École Publique de la Rue du Divan (Algiers), *81*
education: Alliance Israélite Universelle, 29, 33, 116, 117
Egypt: amends to Sephardi Jews, 122–23; anti-Semitism and pogroms, 24, 54, 74–75; in Arab League, 51; Ben Ezra Synagogue (Cairo), 24, *123*; Black Saturday, 69, 71; blockade of Straits of Tiran, 85; British colonial rule, 15–16, 22; Byzantine conquest of Jerusalem and, 14; Eliyahu Hanavi Synagogue (Alexandria), 122, *124*; exodus from, 68, 73–74, 75, 105; First Arab-Israeli War (1948), 55, 58; Free Officers Movement, 71; impact of exodus, 121; interwar period, 23–24; Jewish population, 23, 49, 68, 96, 103; Levon Affair, 71; Maimonides Synagogue (Cairo), 122; Mamluk Egypt, 14; Moses and, 8; Roman Empire and, 12; Six-Day War, 86, *86*, 88–89, *89*; Suez Crisis, *71*, 71–74; Talmud Torah school (Helwan), 24; Yom Kippur War, 96–97, *97*
Elbaz, Edmond, *136*
Eliyahu Hanavi Synagogue (Alexandria, Egypt), 122, *124*
England. *See* United Kingdom
Europe, 14–15. *See also* Ashkenazi Jews; France; Germany; Italy; United Kingdom
Exilarch's Foundation, 113–14
Ezekiel (prophet), 9, *10*
Ezekiel's Tomb, *11*, 114
Ezra (prophet), 11

Faisal (king of Syria, later of Iraq), 20, 22, *26*
Farhud (Iraqi pogrom), 47, *47*–49
Farouk (king of Egypt), 71, *72*
First Arab-Israeli War (War of Independence, 1948), 55, *56*, 58
First Zionist Congress, *16*
Fourth Aliyah, *40*
France: Algerian colonial rule, 33–34, 78–80; Algerian Revolution and, 80–81; anti-Semitism, 114–15; colonial territories in Middle East and North Africa, 3, 15, 20, 22; expulsion of Jews, 15; Sephardi resettlement and contributions, 110, 116–17; Tunisian colonial rule, 34
Free Officers Movement, 71
Front de Libération Nationale (FLN), 80–81, 82

Gaddafi, Muammar, 95
al-Gaylani, Rashid Ali, 42, 47, *47*
Germany: Iraq and, 47; Morocco during WWII and, 46; Nazis, 22, 24, 29, 42;

Ottoman Empire and, 19, 20; in Tunisia during WWII, 45, 46
Ghavitian, Zaki, 41, *41*–42, 101, 103
Gilbert, Martin, 89
Glasberg, Father, *66*, 66–67
Glasser, Juliette Akouka, 69, *69*, 71, *105*
Goren, Shlomo, *86*
Gozlan, Lilian Carmona, *130*
Great Britain. *See* United Kingdom
Great Synagogue (Synagogue de Rue Randon, Algiers), 34, *44*
Green Line (Armistice Line), 57
Guess, 119
Guetta, Beniamino, *95*
Guetta, Ever, *95*
Guetta, Hamos, 36, 94–95, *95*
Guetta, Isacco, *95*
Guetta, Scialom, *95*
Guetta, Tonina Drikes, *95*

Hacohen, David, *52*
Haganah, 64, 66
Haim, Sabah, *90*
Halahmy, Oded, *134*
Halala, Edy Cohen, 98–99, *99*
Halala, Robert Cohen, *99*
Halimi, Alphonse, 120, *120*
Halimi, Gisèle, 119, *119*
Hallak, Nina Rabih, *132*
Harary, Ketti, *77*
Harkabi, Yehoshafat, *58*
Haroche, Serge, 116
Hassan II (king of Morocco), 76
Hazaquiel, David, *90*
Hillel, Shlomo, 64, *64*–67, *65*, *66*, 89, 112, *112*–13
Hitler, Adolf, 24, 29; *Mein Kampf* (Arabic edition), 43
Hungary, 15
Hussein, Saddam, 78, 91, 123
al-Husseini, Amin (Mufti of Jerusalem), *39*, 42, 43, 47, *47*

Iran: anti-Semitism, 41–42, 100–101; exodus from, 68, 101, 103; Iranian Revolution, 42, *102*, 102–3; Jewish integration, 42; Jewish population, 3, 41, 49, 68, 96, 103; shahs' regime, 100; Six-Day War and, 101; Zargar family, 42
Iraq: anti-Semitism and repression, 29, 63, *67*; in Arab League, 51; Baghdad Chamber of Commerce, *26*; British colonial rule, 15, 20, 22, 25; damaged scrolls and other documents recovered by U.S. Army, 7, 123, *124*, *125*; exodus from, 67, 91–93, 105; Farhud pogrom, 47, *47*–49; First Arab-Israeli War (1948) and, 55, 58; impact of exodus, 121; interwar period, 25,

27–28; Jewish population, 3, 28, 49, 68, 96, *103*; Laura Kadoorie Alliance School for Girls (Baghdad), *26*; music, *122*; Operation Ezra and Nehemiah, 64, *64*, 66, 67–68; remaining Jewish population, 106; repression under Ba'ath Party, 76–78, 89–91, *90*, 93; Roman Empire and, 13; smuggling Jews out of, 63–67
Islam: Abraham and, 8; conflict with Jews, 13–14; *dhimmi* status, 14, 16, 19, 25, 29, 34, 40, 41; establishment by Muhammad, 13, *13*; Sephardi Jews under, 1–2. *See also* Arab countries
Ismail, Ahmed, 97
Israel: Armistice Agreements (1949), *58*; Armistice Line (Green Line), 57; collective forgetting of Arabs, 113; establishment, 52, 53, 55; Operation Ezra and Nehemiah, 64, *64*, 66, 67–68; Operation Magic Carpet, 58, *59*, 60–61; Palestinian Arabs and, 2, 57, 58, 89, 110–11; pogroms in response to, 53–54; refugee resettlement challenges, 106–7; Sephardi contributions, 117–18; Sephardi resettlement, 105–6, 107, 109–10, *112*; Six-Day War, 86, *86*, 88–89, *89*, 95, 101; tensions with Arab countries, 51, 52, 53, 85; War of Independence (1948), 55, *56*, 58; Yom Kippur War, 96–97, *97*, 98. *See also* Palestine
Italy, 22, 35, 45
Itzhak, Ibrahim Haim Moallem, *26*

Jaffa (Palestine), *39*
Jeremiah (prophet), 9
Jerusalem, 8, 9, 11, 13, 20, 38, 39, 56. *See also* Israel; Palestine
Jesus, 12–13. *See also* Christianity
Jewish Legion, 21
Jews: about, 7; Abraham, 7–8; Alexander the Great and, 11–12; Assyrians and, *10*; Babylonian captivity and return from exile, 9, 11; Byzantine Empire and, 13, 15; Christianity and, 12–13, 14–15; *dhimmi* status, 14, 16, 19, 25, 29, 34, 40, 41; in Europe, 14–15; Islam and, 1–2, 13–14; Israelite monarchy, 8; Moses, 8; Ottoman Empire and, 15–16; Persians and, 13; Roman Empire and, 12, *12*, 13; Western civilization and, 8–9; Zionism, 16, 17, 20, 37, 42, 111. *See also* Israel; Palestine; Sephardi Jews; *specific countries*
jizya tax, 14, 41
Jordan: in Arab League, 51; establishment, 22; First Arab-Israeli War (1948) and, 55, 58; Palestinian Arabs and, 110; Six-Day War and, 86; tensions with Israel, 85

Josielewski, Mary Judah-Jacob, 58, 60, *60*, 113, *113*

Kane, Betty Bivas, *130*
Kaplan, Cynthia Shamash, *135*
Karsenti, Michéle Hagege, *126*, *128*
Kashi, Dhiaa Kasim, 121, *121*
Kassab, Toufik, 54, *54*, 77
Katab, Yitzhak, 60–61, *61*
Keslassy, Simon, *126*, *136*
el-Keslassy family (Morocco), *53*
Kessar, Israel, 117
El-Kevity, Shlomo, *109*, 109–10
Khalifa, Robert, 73, 74, *107*
Al Khederi, Mohammed Kamel, 26
Khomeini, Ayatollah, 42, *102*, *102*
Kojaman, Yeheskel, *134*
Kurdish Jews, 28
Al Kuwaity, Saleh, *109*, 122

Labi, Aldo, *36*
Labi, Ghita, *36*
Labi, Moshe, 35, *35*, *36*, 45–46
L'Antijuif algérien (newspaper), 34
Lasry, John, *129*
Laura Kadoorie Alliance School for Girls (Baghdad), 26
Lawrence, T.E., 22
Lebanon: anti-Semitism, 98–99; in Arab League, 51; civil war, 98; escape from Syria via, 68, 94; First Arab–Israeli War (1948) and, 55, 58; French colonial rule, 20, 22; Jewish population, 49, 68, 96, 103
Levon Affair, 71
Levy, Albert, *131*
Lévy, Bernard-Henri, *116*, *116*
Levy, David, 117
Libya: anti-Semitism and pogroms, 51, 94–95; exodus from, 68, 95; First Arab–Israeli War (1948) and, 55; interwar period, 35–36; Italian colonial rule, 22, 35–36; Jewish population, 3, 35, 49, 68, 96, *103*; Roman Empire and, 12; Six-Day War and, 88, 95; WWII and, 45–46
Lieberman, Noemi, *129*
Lopez, Tomas, *126*

Mackintosh-Smith, Tim, 17
Maimonides, 14, *14*
Maimonides Synagogue (Cairo, Egypt), 122
Mamluk Egypt, 14
Marciano, Paul, *119*
Marzouk, Moussa, *70*
Mashaal, Edna Gareh, 110, *111*
Mashaal, Robert, *135*
Mashaal, Victor, 25, *25*, 121
Meghira, Abraham, 19
Meir, Ruth, *133*
Memmi, Albert, 106, *106*

Mizrahi Jews, 3. *See also* Sephardi Jews
Mohammad Reza Pahlavi (shah of Iran), 100
Mohammed V (king of Morocco), 46, *46*
Mohammed VI (king of Morocco), 121
Moncef Bey (bey of Tunis), 46, *46*
Morocco: amends to Sephardi Jews, 121; anti-Semitism, 29, 32, 43; École de l'Alliance Israélite (Tétouan), 31; exodus from, 76, 98, 105; First Arab–Israeli War (1948) and, 55; French colonial rule, 22, 29; interwar period, 29; Jewish population, 3, 29, 49, 68, 96, 103; Joan of Arc celebration, 31; photographs of Jews, *1*, *30*, *31*, *75*; Roman Empire and, 12; Six-Day War and, 86; WWII and, 43, 46; Yom Kippur War and, 98
Moses, 8, 9
Mossad, 71, 76
Mossad LeAliyah Bet, 63
Mufti of Jerusalem (Amin al-Husseini), 39, 42, 43, 47, *47*
Muhammad, 13, *13*
Muslim Brotherhood, 24, 69, 71

Nacamulli, Alec, 122
Nahmad, David, 120
Nakba, 58
Nasser, Gamal Abdel, 70, 71, 85
nationalism, Arab, 17, 19, 20, 22. *See also* Arab countries
Nazis, 22, 24, 29, 42, 46, 47
Nebuchadnezzar (king of Babylon), 9
Neguib, Muhammad, 71
Nehemiah (prophet), 11

el-Okbi, Taieb, 46
Operation Ezra and Nehemiah, 64, *64*, *66*, 67–68
Operation Magic Carpet, 58, *59*, 60–61
Organisation de l'Armée Secrète (OAS), 81, 82
Organization of the Oppressed on Earth, 99
Ottoman Empire, 15–16, 19–20, *20*
Ovadia, Rose, *129*

Palestine: Arab opposition to Jewish statehood, 51, *52*, 53–54; Balfour Declaration, 20, *22*, 24, 42; British colonial rule, 20, 22, 39; Jewish-Arab conflict, 37, *38*, *39*, 39, 42; mason in Tel Aviv, *37*; partition plan, 53, *53*; WWI and, *21*; Zionist settlement, 20, 37. *See also* Israel
Palestine Post (newspaper), 55
Palestinian Arabs, 2, *57*, 58, 89, 110–11
Paris Peace Conference, 20, 22, 39
Peres, Shimon, 68
Persian Jews, 3. *See also* Iran

Persians, 13
Pfizer, 120
Portugal, 15

Rabba, Ines, *95*
Rabin, Yitzhak, *58*
Reza Khan (shah of Iran), 100
Roman Empire, 12, *12*, 13
Roosevelt, Franklin D., 46

al-Sabawi, Yunis, 47; *Mein Kampf* (Hitler) translation, 43
Sabet, Rolen, *131*
Sadat, Anwar, 97
Safwat, Ahmed, 77, *78*
Salama, Eva, *72*
Salih, Khalda, *106*
Samimy, Lina Zargar, *100*, 100–101, *101*
Sarajevo Haggadah (manuscript), *9*
Saudi Arabia, 51
Saul (king of Israel), 8
Scemama, Elisa Diaine, 114–15, *115*
Sephardi Jews (Arab Jews): about, 1–2, 3–4, 17, 125, 127; amends from Arab countries, 121–23; Arab League against, 51, 53, 54; contributions in new homes, 106, 112–20; *dhimmi* status, 14, 16, 19, 25, 29, 34, 40, 41; exodus of, 58, 68, 69, 89, 105; impact of exodus on Arab countries, 120–21; lack of international support, 110, 111–12; lack of truth and reconciliation from Arab countries, 125; pogroms against after creation of Israel, 53–54; populations in 10 Islamic countries, 49, 68, 96, *103*; Portrait Gallery, 127; reluctance to discuss past, 117; resettlement in Israel, 105–6, 107, 109–10, 112; resettlement in West, 110; use of terms, 3; during WWII, 42–43, 45–49; Zionism and, 17. *See also specific countries*
Sephardi Voices International (SVI), 2
Septuagint, 12
Shahmoon, Sassoon, *135*
Shama, David, 71–74, *72*, 114
Shama, Isaac, *72*
Sharet, Moshe, *52*
Sharp, Liam, *126*
Shazli, Sadedin, 97
Shem-Tov, Yehezkel, 67
Shohet, Hillel, *133*
Shohet, Maurice, *134*
Shohet, Violet-Albertine, 51
Shuker, Edwin, 89–92, *91*, *92*, 114, *114*
Sidi, Robert, *132*
Silver, Vivianne, *131*
Simon, Arieh, 58
Sitbon, Channah Ankri, 45, *45*
Six-Day War, 86, *86*, 88–89, *89*, 95, 101
Snowdin, Fortuna, *95*
Solomon (king of Israel), 8

Sourani, Sami, 48, *48*
Spain, 14, 15
Straits of Tiran, 85
Suez Crisis, *71*, 71-74
al-Suwaidi, Tawfiq, 67
Syria: anti-Semitism and pogroms, 54,
    98; in Arab League, 51; emigration
    and other restrictions, 76, 93-94, 97;
    exodus from, 68; First Arab-Israeli
    War (1948) and, 55, 58; French colonial
    rule, 20, 22; interwar period, 36-37;
    Jewish population, *49*, *68*, *96*, *103*;
    Six-Day War and, 86; Yom Kippur
    War and, 96, 97

Talmud, 11
Tanakh, 9
Tanzimat reforms, 16
Tawfik, Gabrielle Elia, 93-94, *94*
Tlass, Mustafa, 98
Torah: burial of damaged Torah from
    Iraq, 123, *124*; creation of, 9; Sephardi
    vs. Ashkenazi reading practices, 3;
    translation into Greek, 12
Tripoli (Libya), 35, 55, 88, 95
truth and reconciliation, 125
Tunisia: exodus from, 75-76; French
    colonial rule, 15, 22, 34; interwar
    period, 34; Jewish population, 3, 34,
    49, *68*, *96*, *103*; Roman Empire and, 12;
    WWII and, 43, 44, 45, 46

United Kingdom: Arab opposition to, 42;
    Balfour Declaration, 20, 22, 24, 42;
    colonial territories in Middle East and
    North Africa, 15-16, 22; expulsion of
    Jews, 15; in Iraq, 25; in Palestine, 20,
    38, *39*; Sephardi contributions to,
    113-14
United Nations, 67, 96, 98, 111-12
United Nations Relief and Works Agency
    (UNRWA), 2, 110-11
Universal Declaration of Human Rights, 117
Urbach, Flo Dahoud, *133*

Wahnich, Emile, 29, 32, *32*
Wahnich, Ninette, *32*
Wahnich, Simy, *32*
War of Independence (First Arab-Israeli
    War, 1948), 55, *56*, 58
Weisel, Eli, 125
Western civilization, 8-9
World Islamic Congress, 89
World War I, 19-20, *20*, *21*. *See also* Paris
    Peace Conference
World War II, 42-43, *43*, *44*, 45-47

Yadin, Yigal, *58*
Yefet, Shalom, *129*
Yemen: anti-Semitism, 40; in Arab League,
    51; Jewish population, 40, *49*, *68*, *96*,

103; Jewish resettlement in Israel, *40*,
    62, 110; Operation Magic Carpet, 58,
    59, 60-61; refugees with Torah, *vi*. *See
    also* Aden
Yom Kippur War, 96-97, *97*, 98
Yom Plittim, 118
Yusef, Jakob, *106*
Yuval, Mike, *135*

Zagury, Joseph, *137*
Zamir, Levana Vidal, 23, *23*, 24
Zamir-Belbel, Ezra, 24
Zargar, Shahverdi, *42*
Zargar family (Iran), *42*
Zelouf, Aida Basri, *134*
Zilkha, Abdulla, *29*
Zilkha, Ezra, 27-28, *28*, 29
Zilkha, Khedouri, *29*
Zilkha, Maurice, *29*
Zilkha, Selim, *29*
Zilkha Bank (Baghdad), 27, *28*, 29
Zionism, *16*, 17, 20, 37, 42, 111

ABOUT THE AUTHORS

HENRY GREEN is Professor of Religious Studies and the former director of Judaic and Sephardic Studies at the University of Miami, Florida. He is the founding director of MOSAIC: the Jewish Museum of Florida, and of Sephardi Voices, an audiovisual digital archive of Arab Jews. He has served as a Visiting Fellow at Oxford University and at the Hebrew University of Jerusalem, and has given testimony to the Congressional Human Rights Caucus in the United States as an advocate for the rights of those displaced.

RICHARD STURSBERG is the author of *The Tower of Babble* (2012), named by the *Globe and Mail* (Canada's national newspaper) as one of the best books of the year; and *The Tangled Garden* (2019), which was shortlisted for Canada's Donner Prize for the best book on public policy. He is the president of PEN Canada and chairman of Sephardi Voices International.